THE
ASSURED
PATHWAY
TO THE
MIRACULOUS

Sam Adelusimo

The Assured Pathway to The Miraculous

Published by Cornerstone Publishing
A Division of Cornerstone Creativity Group LLC
Info@thecornerstonepublishers.com
www.thecornerstonepublishers.com

Author's Contact
To book the author to speak at your next event or to order bulk copies of this book, please, use the information below:
adelusimo@gmail.com

Printed in the United States of America.

Dedication

To my Lord and Savior, the Lord Jesus Christ, who made Himself a sacrifice for me and gave me the most important miracle in heaven and on earth.

To my precious wife and children. For your unquantifiable sacrifices day and night through the years as we navigate the journeys of life and ministry together. I remain indebtedly grateful to each and all of you.

To Late Brother Banji, fondly called "Coke or Coca-Cola" of Christ Apostolic Church, Oke Iyin Akure, Nigeria. I doubt that anyone reading this book will know you, but I am grateful to you for introducing Jesus Christ to me. Continue to rest in the Lord.

Contents

Acknowledgments

I have always desired to write books. There has been a specific prophecy and word of knowledge that the grace to write books is upon my life, but there have been unexplainable challenges along the way. However, my publisher, Cornerstone Publishing, led by Pastor Gbenga Showunmi, a man who does not believe in impossibilities, has made the dream come true! I am extremely grateful to you and your team!

Introduction

One major avenue through which God has consistently demonstrated His sovereignty over the universe is His timely interventions in the affairs of mankind. While it is true that God has placed man on the earth to be in charge of His creation, it is also true that man cannot totally figure out the complexities of life or navigate all of its challenges on his own. From time to time, we are faced with issues and situations that only the omnipotent power of God can solve. And as many generations of mankind can testify, God has always proved to be both able and willing to solve even the most perplexing of human challenges.

However, beyond being regular recipients of His miraculous power, God actually wants us to be supercharged carriers and dispensers of this power for miracles to the world around us. He wants us to consistently function in the realm of the miraculous because it is one of the most compelling proofs our being His children and true representatives on earth.

Especially in these days of increased global crises, personal struggles, and feelings of uncertainty, the need for miracles and the miraculous has never been more pressing. Unfortunately, however, the vast majority of people seeking miracles and the miraculous are either not following the right way or somewhat ignorant of the only assured (fully guaranteed or fail-proof) pathway. This pathway is God's Word.

God's Word is not merely a collection of ancient texts; it is a living, breathing testament to His enduring love, wisdom, and supernatural interventions throughout history. Within its verses lie the keys to unlocking the boundless treasures of God's promises and miraculous power. Amidst the uncertainty, unrest and unfathomable experiences of life, God's Word stands as an unshakable refuge and a beacon of light towards a life infused with the miraculous.

This book is an exploration into this unparalleled power that is embedded within the sacred Scriptures. Through personal testimonies and biblical examples, we will be reminded that our God is a God of miracles and that there is nothing too big or too small for Him to handle. The book will also delve into how we can become spiritual giants that daily enjoy and transmit God's miraculous power for the benefit of humanity and the advancement of God's kingdom.

My prayer for you, dear reader, is that your journey

through the pages of this book and, more importantly, through the sacred Scriptures, will awaken within you a renewed hunger and thirst for God's Word. This will serve as a catalyst for your own miracles, as well as the release of God's unfailing power upon the multitudes of others around you.

1

MIRACLES STILL HAPPEN

"Miracle is God suspending natural laws and personally reaching into life to rearrange people and their circumstances according to His will." - **John MacArthur**

"And Jesus went about all Galilee, teaching in their synagogues, preaching the gospel of the kingdom, and healing all kinds of sickness and all kinds of disease among the people. Then His fame went throughout all Syria; and they brought to Him all sick people who were afflicted with various diseases and torments, and those who were demon-possessed, epileptics, and paralytics; and He healed them." - *(Matthew 4:23-24)*

"Jesus Christ is the same yesterday, today, and forever."- *(Hebrews 13:8)*

Miracles are God's supernatural interventions in the natural affairs of mankind. The keywords here are "supernatural" and "interventions". Miracles are supernatural because they defy natural and scientific explanations. They are occurrences that shatter the most reliable of human predictions, the most established of scientific theories and the most unchangeable of natural laws.

Miracles are divine "interventions" because they often have to do with situations that are beyond human ability and control. The dictionary defines "intervention" as the act of interfering with the outcome or course especially of a condition or process (as to prevent harm or improve functioning). This makes it clear that miracles are God's timely and unfailing "interferences" that make possible what is naturally, humanly, and scientifically impossible.

The word "miracle" comes from the Greek thaumasion and the Latin miraculum - both of which refer to "that which causes wonder and astonishment, being extraordinary in itself and amazing or inexplicable by normal standards." God is the specialist in miracles because it is through miracles that His supremacy and sovereignty over the universe are most demonstrated. In other words, miracles are His way of showing that even though there are established natural laws, scientific principles, societal norms and even dreaded supernatural forces, He is the one with the ultimate authority over every twist and turn of the universe.

The Holman Bible Dictionary defines miracles as "events which unmistakably involve an immediate and powerful action of God designed to reveal His character or purposes." It is also for this reason that miracles, in biblical language, are also referred to as "signs" and "wonders". Miracles are signs because they do not just happen for the sake of it; they happen to point attention to God and to validate the ministrations of His ministers – especially to unbelievers. They are wonders because they describe God's supernatural abilities and represent special manifestations of His power. Other words used to denote miracles in the Scripture include "works" (Matthew 11:2; John 14:12), "mighty works" (Matthew 13:58) and "power" or "dunamis" (Acts 1:8).

I am hoping that the background being laid here will stir your faith towards seeing and experiencing God's mighty works in an unprecedented dimension in your life, career, or ministry. Whatever your present situation is or whatever reports or diagnoses you may have received, I see God rearranging every aspect of your life and destiny from this moment with His mighty works in Jesus' precious name. I see Him demonstrating His omnipotence in your life and situation to cause a change of outcome in every situation that currently baffles or frightens you, in Jesus' name.

MIRACLES AROUND THE WORLD

*"...all the earth shall be filled with the glory of the LORD" (**Numbers 14:21**).*

*"And the disciples went everywhere and preached, and the Lord worked through them, confirming what they said by many miraculous signs" (**Mark 16:20, NLT**)*

In addition to the above fundamental truths about miracles, let me briefly share with you two major instances of divine interventions in people's lives that gained worldwide attention, shook the scientific community, and confounded even the most adamant of atheists.

At about 10:30 on the night of March 6, 2015, 25-year-old Lynn Jennifer Groesbeck, who was returning from visiting her parents, lost control of her car and landed in the icy Spanish Fork River, in Utah. Sadly, nobody knew of the accident, until over 13 hours later, the next day. A fisherman had sighted the upturned car, partially submerged in the river, and immediately dialed 911. Soon after, police officers and firefighters were at the scene.

Looking at the car's wreckage and considering the freezing temperature of the river, these first responders didn't expect to see any survivors. And truly, when they managed to reach the car, they found Lynn in the driver seat, long dead. In fact, as the medical examiner would later reveal, she had died almost immediately, as a result of blunt force injury of the head.

Seeing no one else, the officers concluded that the rescue mission was over. But then, they soon began to hear the voice of an adult woman calling for help from the same car. That seemed strange because there was no one else in sight. However, as the "help me" plea persisted, the officers were prompted to double-check. They flipped the car over, and right before them was an amazing sight. Strapped to the seat in the back of the car was Lilly, Lynn's 18-month-old daughter. She had been hanging upside down for 14 hours in freezing temperatures without being dressed for the cold. She was, in fact, wearing only a flannel onesie.

A firefighter jumped into the river and cut the car-seat straps, freeing Lilly, who was unconscious but alive. Officers then formed a line in the river and handed the cold child from one person to the next, until she was on the shoreline and in emergency workers' arms. Thereafter, she was taken into the waiting ambulance, where CPR was performed on her. By Monday, she had recovered quite rapidly and would go on to recover fully soon afterwards.

Lilly's case so astounded America that she was dubbed "the miracle baby". The questions on the lips of everyone were:

- *How did Lilly survive dangling upside-down for over 14 hours, while so flimsily dressed in such an icy river?* By the way, the river was so cold that the rescue crew members could only stay in for short periods of time. In fact, after the rescue, some of the officers had to be taken to the hospital to be treated for hypothermia.

- *How did Lilly survive the freezing temperatures throughout the night and for most of the next morning?*

- *Who directed that fisherman to that part of the river at that particular time of the day?* Keep in mind that although the road that goes over the bridge gets plenty of traffic, the view below was obstructed by the cement barrier above. This was why no one saw the car for several hours, and it could have been that way for much longer).

- Most importantly, *whose voice did the first responding officers – three police officers and two firemen - hear calling for help?*

To show that "the voice" that the officers heard was not mere hallucination, all of the five first respondents actually attested to hearing it. One of the officers, Jared Warner, said: "It wasn't just in our heads. To me, it was plain as day. I remember hearing a voice that didn't sound like a child, just saying 'help me'." Similarly, Spanish Fork Police Officer, Tyler Beddoes, said, "Someone said 'help me' inside that car... It's a miracle...Knowing that she was trapped in there 14 hours, the cold water running through car, just blows me away."

By the mercies of the merciful God, may the voice of miracle cry out for you and your household whenever you need it in Jesus' name.

As previously mentioned, throughout the United States, and in other parts of the world, where the news of Lilly's survival and rescue was reported, even the most unreligious could not but admit that it was a divine intervention! This immediately reminds me of Psalm 126:1-2, which says, "*When the LORD turned again the captivity of Zion, we were like them that dream. Then was our mouth filled with laughter, And our tongue with singing: Then said they among the heathen, The LORD hath done great things for them...*"

I pray that your own miracle and testimonies shall be the next for the world to hear in Jesus' name. The miracle-working God will do something mighty in your life that will make even "the heathen" around you to acknowledge His existence and wonder-working power.

INCREDIBLE RECOVERY

On June 7, 2014, 30-year-old Grayson Kirby and his friend were participating in a demolition derby at the Mid-Atlantic Power Festival in Ruckersville, Greene County, Virginia, when their vehicle hit a rock, flipped over, and Grayson was violently thrown out. He was thrown so far that it was difficult finding him. When rescuers eventually located him at the bottom of a hill, he was in a very terrible condition. First, he was not breathing and had no pulse for about seven minutes. Second, almost every bone in his body was broken. Thus, by the time he was rushed to the University of Virginia Medical Center, he was technically dead.

After frantically battling for some minutes, the medics were able to get Grayson breathing again with a life support machine. His condition, however, remained so bad that doctors did not really expect him to survive. His injuries were extensive. Aside from his broken bones, his lungs were crushed, and he had internal bleeding and significant head trauma. His brain also suffered multiple strokes and his kidneys were failing.

Immediately Grayson's parents (Wayne and Karen) heard details of the accident through a phone call, they figured that it was a case that was hopeless with human effort. Therefore, even as they feared the worst before leaving the house, they took time to pray and asked God to take control of the situation. When they eventually got to the hospital, what they saw broke them down completely. According to Karen, "To see my son lying there, so swollen; he was unrecognizable. Tubes in all parts of his body. I was in shock. As a mother, you want to fix it. But I couldn't fix it; I couldn't do anything. My son was dying and we had nowhere to go but on our knees and just pray to God."

Doctors actually told Grayson's parents he had less than 2 per cent chance of survival, meaning that they were very likely to lose him. Though devastated, the parents did not lose hope. They informed their Christian brethren and other Christians in their community. Thousands of people in the community and beyond kept Grayson in their thoughts and prayers and wore red shirts designed to show support for the injured man. Information was also sent out through social media, requesting for prayers.

After some days of prayer, Grayson's oxygen level started to improve. He was consequently taken off life support and placed in a medically induced coma. However, MRI scan soon showed that he had suffered several strokes and a brain hemorrhage. This proved to be another devastating blow. His mother recalled that moment, saying, "I'll never forget the doctor's face when he was talking. He couldn't even look at us; he was looking at the floor as he was talking to us. He said if Grayson ever woke up, it would be up to two months and there was no telling what would be in his brain. And I remember asking him, 'You mean he'll be a vegetable?' That got us really devastated because we had believed that he was improving but now we were hearing that he might never wake up and if he did he might never have any brain function. So I had to start praying again."

After about ten days, the first of the prayers of God's people was answered - Grayson opened his eyes. Soon after, he began mouthing a question about the whereabouts of his friend, with whom he had been in the vehicle (who luckily survived with minor injuries). Karen recalled, "We knew at that point that he was in there" – referring to his brain function.

Wayne also said, "After Grayson woke up, we realized that God was in control, and it didn't matter what the doctor said to us, God is the Master Physician, and it's His will that would be done. Within hours, he mouthed the correct answer to every question the hospital staff asked. The doctors were speechless. He was soon on his way to recovery."

Indeed, the doctors were amazed, but they were still doubtful that Grayson would ever be able to walk or talk normally again. Still, the family continued to pray, and God continued to heal Grayson gradually, till he surpassed all the milestones set by his caregivers. Grayson himself recalls, "Things just kept getting better, progressing every day."

After two months of rehab and therapy, Grayson was cleared to go home. All his organs had regained their functions, and he could walk and talk normally again. He had become completely whole through the power of prayer.

As I write, doctors still find it difficult to explain Grayson's miraculous recovery. A doctor particularly said of his case: "There's no other case I've ever seen that was as extreme an example as this - that had as poor a prognosis as Grayson had and has recovered as much as he has."

I decree, once again, that you will experience God's divine powerful intervention in your life – one that will cause such a mighty turnaround in your health, finances, family, business and ministry that will make everyone around you to glorify God for you and want to make them to serve your God.

THE MESSAGE

Why did I share these two life-rescue-ing testimonies?

I narrated the above miracles, not because they are the most spectacular in contemporary times but because they are two of the most recent in public domain and therefore can be easily verified by anyone. The deeper message here, however, is that multitudes of miracles still happen every day that prove that our God, indeed, reigns and rules in the affairs of men. While some of these miracles have become so routine that we sometimes take them for granted (prompting the caution in Psalm 103:2), some are so remarkable that we just cannot but be awed by God's awesomeness.

I considered it necessary to begin our journey in this book on this note (examining the concept of miracle in itself) because if we do not establish and reinforce our faith in the supernatural power of God to perform wonders, moving to the rest of the chapters – which include operating in the miraculous and mastering the keys to the miraculous - will be pointless. You see, the world today is under such a critical siege of widespread unbelief and skepticism about spiritual matters. More than ever before, the kingdom of Satan is bent on wrecking people's faith in God and diverting humanity's attention to trifles.

The onslaught against believing in the miracles and the wonder-working power of the Lord is being driven by three main factors. The first is the increasing spread of misleading ideas from godless scientists and desperate atheists. The second is the stench of the atrocities being committed by some false ministers of God in the name of performing miracles. Last but not the least is the barrage of personal challenges confronting believers in Christ in this perilous period. Simply put, we are currently living in that particular time about which Christ predicted, *"When the Son of man cometh, shall he find faith on the earth?"* (Luke 18:8).

As you look around too, you may notice the signs that justify this vital question that our Lord asked thousands of years ago. Many people are indeed "departing from the faith, giving heed to seducing spirits and doctrines of devils." (1 Timothy 4:1-2). There are even some that appear to still be in the faith but are having deep doubts about the possibility of divine interventions and the supremacy of God over events in the world. Therefore, even though my ultimate goal in this book is to show you the assured pathway to the miraculous, my first mission here is to assure you that we serve a miracle-working God, who is the same yesterday, today and forever. Therefore, be assured that whatever challenge you may be having, the Almighty God that we serve knows no limitation or impossibility (Matthew 19:26). From this moment, in your life, *"every valley shall be filled, and every mountain and hill shall be brought low; and the crooked shall be made straight, and the rough ways shall be made smooth."* (Luke 3:5).

2

CLARIFYING MISCONCEPTIONS ON SEEKING MIRACLES

"Christianity is a faith that is based upon and rooted in miracles. Take away miracles, and you take away Christianity." – **R.C. Sproul**

"Many are the afflictions of the righteous, But the LORD delivers him out of them all." **(Psalms 34:19)**

"Is anyone among you sick? Let him call for the elders of the church, and let them pray over him, anointing him with oil in the name of the Lord. And the prayer of faith will save the sick, and the Lord will raise him up."
(James 5:14-15)

Charles Haddon Spurgeon is generally regarded as one of the greatest ministers of the gospel that God blessed humanity with in the last century. Yet, as many who were close to him would readily affirm, he was a man acquainted with afflictions. At one time, during a sermon, he shared the following testimony:

"When I was racked some months ago with pain, to an extreme degree, so that I could no longer bear it without crying out, I asked all to go from the room, and leave me alone; and then I had nothing I could say to God but this, 'Thou art my Father, and I am thy child; and thou, as a Father, art tender and full of mercy. I could not bear to see my child suffer as thou makest me suffer, and if I saw him tormented as I am now, I would do what I could to help him, and put my arms under him to sustain him. Wilt thou hide thy face from me, my Father? ... So I pleaded, and I ventured to say, when I was quiet, and they came back who watched me: 'I shall never have such pain again from this moment, for God has heard my prayer.' I bless God that ease came and the racking pain never returned."

The story referenced above is for the purpose of examining a vital issue that we cannot but address as we progress on our journey to the assured pathway to the miraculous. It is not uncommon to find people who hold the view that having a challenge or difficulty that requires divine intervention is a sign of being an unbeliever or an errant believer, who is under divine punishment. As far as such people are concerned, needing or seeking a miracle is something shameful because it connotes that the seeker is either a weak Christian or one suffering the repercussions of sin committed by him or someone from his or her lineage.

These are erroneous views that completely contradict the position of the Scripture. Interestingly, the disciples of Jesus themselves, once found themselves in such a web of misconception, until the Master had to open their eyes. *"And as Jesus passed by, he saw a man which was blind from his birth. And his disciples asked him, saying, Master, who did sin, this man, or his parents, that he was born blind? Jesus answered, Neither hath this man sinned, nor his parents: but that the works of God should be made manifest in him."* (John 9:1-3).

Jesus Christ, by this declaration, clarified that miracles over challenges of life are an integral part of God's design for our lives on earth. This is to say that seeking miracles is a normal part of human life, in general, and the Christian life, in particular. We cannot do without seeking divine interventions in the different aspects of our lives from time to time. The first reason for this, as our introductory quote and scriptures show, is that Christianity itself is rooted in miracles. This means that without miracles there wouldn't be Christianity in the first place. If this surprises you, then try to recall our definition of miracles in the previous chapter.

Everything about our faith and our lives as children of

God is a miracle. Take the incarnation of Christ, which is the foundation of our faith, as an example. It is the greatest of all miracles. Or how do you explain God being born in human form – and through a virgin – if not a miracle? As Paul the apostle says in 1 Timothy 3:16, "And without controversy great is the mystery of godliness: God was manifest in the flesh, justified in the Spirit, seen of angels, preached unto the Gentiles, believed on in the world, received up into glory."

Our coming into God's Kingdom through salvation is also miracle – that is, it is something that could never have happened without divine intervention. *"For by grace are ye saved through faith; and that not of yourselves: it is the gift of God: not of works, lest any man should boast."* (Ephesians 2:8-9). Writing on this, Jim Eliff explains, "Our salvation is a miraculous intervention of God. Evangelism is all about miracles. We pray asking God to change the human will, or to override and arrange the natural course of things in certain ways, or to defy all odds." St. Augustine, too, expressed a similar view, using his personal experience, "I never have any difficulty believing in miracles, since I experienced the miracle of a change in my own heart."

On and on, we can highlight why other elements of our faith are miraculous but my point here is to remove the misconception that seeking miracles is an anomaly for a believer. King David, despite being a "man after God's heart", reflected on his life's journey, as well as the experiences of others, and declared by divine inspiration that *"many are the afflictions of the righteous: but the LORD delivereth him out of them all."* (Psalm 34:19).

Similarly, all through the Scripture, we find several instances of God's people either seeking miracles or performing the miraculous for their own benefit or their benefit or others. I will mention a good number of such in the next chapter. Notwithstanding, mentioning a few here will help. Lazarus is described as a much-beloved friend of Jesus in John 11:3, yet the same verse reveals that he fell gravely ill. A similar thing is said of Epaphroditus, in Philippians 2. Despite being described by Paul as a "brother, and companion in labor, and fellowsoldier", he was also said to have been "sick nigh unto death: but God had mercy on him" (Philippians 2:25-27). Even Paul, the great apostle, had an excruciating burden, for which he persistently sought divine intervention. According to him, *"And lest I should be exalted above measure through the abundance of the revelations, there was given to me a thorn in the flesh, the messenger of Satan to buffet me, lest I should be exalted above measure. For this thing I besought the Lord thrice, that it might depart from me. And he said unto me, My grace is sufficient for thee: for my strength is made perfect in weakness. Most gladly therefore will I rather glory in my infirmities, that the power of Christ may rest upon me."* (2 Corinthians 12:7-9).

Most instructively, our Lord Jesus Christ performed a miracle to meet an urgent financial need for Himself and Peter, in Matthew 17. *"And when they were come to Capernaum, they that received tribute money came to Peter, and said, Doth not your master pay tribute? He saith, Yes. And when he was come into the house, Jesus prevented him, saying, What thinkest thou, Simon? of whom do the kings of the earth take custom or tribute? of their own children, or of strangers? Peter saith unto him, Of strangers. Jesus saith unto him, Then are the children free. Notwithstanding, lest we should offend them, go thou to the sea, and cast an hook, and take up the fish that first cometh up; and when thou hast opened his mouth, thou shalt find a piece of money: that take, and give unto them for me and thee."* (Matthew 17:24-27).

It is not natural to find money in the mouth of a fish. Therefore, even Jesus needed a personal miracle, while on earth. And the situation remains the same till today. Both the high and the low require miraculous interventions to survive the vicissitudes of life and fulfil their destiny. Abraham Lincoln, who is regarded as one of the most successful presidents of the United States, once admitted: "I have been driven many times upon my knees by the overwhelming conviction that I had nowhere else to go. My own wisdom and that of all about me seemed insufficient for that day."

Put your mind at rest therefore and don't let anyone mislead you into believing that the delay, disappointment, setback or sickness for which you are expecting God's miraculous intervention is a sign that you are fallen or forsaken. Your situation does not make you less of a Christian; rather, as Jesus said of the blind man, it only makes you a channel through which God's majesty is manifested, and His name is glorified, even among the heathen. By God's miraculous acts in your life, you shall have testimonies over every challenge, in Jesus' name.

ALL MIRACLES ARE YOURS

Here is something even more gladdening. Not only is God ABLE to meet you at your present area of need but He is actually WILLING to lavish on you as many miracles as you will ever need. You know why? Your being blessed brings glory to His name. No wonder Romans 8:32 declares, *"He that spared not his own Son, but delivered him up for us all, how shall he not with him also freely give us all things?"* God has manifold miracles in store for you. If He can give you the greatest miracle ever – His Son, Jesus Christ, for your redemption - then there is nothing else that can be too big for Him to do for you.

21

The gift of JESUS is the best and mother of all miracles. We must all remember that it is not just salvation that Christ died for. His death brought us all forms of miracles – healing, health, prosperity, and dominion.

By reading and connecting (in faith) with the insights and revelations of the insights and revelations in this book, you are already receiving your miracle. Why did I say this? Every time the word of God is being taught a miracle is taking place. The Bible confirms this. In Luke 5:17, for example, we are told, *"And it came to pass on a certain day, as he was teaching, that there were Pharisees and doctors of the law sitting by, which were come out of every town of Galilee, and Judaea, and Jerusalem: and the power of the Lord was present to heal them."* I can assure you that the unfailing and unchanging miraculous power of God is currently available to not only heal you of any infirmity but to also supply every need you may have.

And do you know one other interesting and assuring thing? Even unbelievers enjoy God's miraculous interventions in their lives. This, as has been hinted earlier, is why miracles are also called "signs". If God makes unbelievers to experience His mighty power, so as to draw them to Him, how much more you who have already become His child by redemption!

Matthew 4:23-25 gives us a glimpse into the all-inclusive

reach of God's miracle power. *"And Jesus went about all Galilee, teaching in their synagogues, and preaching the gospel of the kingdom, and healing all manner of sickness and all manner of disease among the people. And his fame went throughout all Syria: and they brought unto him all sick people that were taken with divers diseases and torments, and those which were possessed with devils, and those which were lunatic, and those that had the palsy; and he healed them. And there followed him great multitudes of people from Galilee, and from Decapolis, and from Jerusalem, and from Judaea, and from beyond Jordan."*

Jesus went about Galilee, not only teaching and preaching but also healing all kinds of diseases and delivering people from all forms of demonic possession. Most of these beneficiaries of Christ's healing touch were not religious people, much less having a covenant relationship with God. And if God can be so merciful as to be interested in the wholeness of such people, you can be sure that He is much more concerned about your wellbeing, fruitfulness, progress and prosperity.

Now, as we close the curtain on this chapter, let me tell you what may be the most surprising and most assuring truth you have heard in a long while. All the miracles you will ever need have been performed already by God. Or let me put it even more strongly – all the miracles that humanity will ever need have been performed by

23

God and can be found on the pages of the Scripture. Therefore, God does not have to start performing a fresh miracle. The great "buffet" of miracles (containing any kind of miracle you may need) is already fully prepared for you in God's word. It is for you to decide which one suits your condition and claim it for your benefit.

Let's dig into some of these miracles, before we explore the keys for actualizing them!

3

CHRONICLES OF MIRACLES FOR YOUR WELLBEING

"Jehovah is the great Miracle Maker, the unrivaled Wonder worker. None can be likened unto Him, He is alone in wonderland, the Creator and Worker of true marvels…" – **C.H. Spurgeon**

"For whatever things were written before were written for our learning, that we through the patience and comfort of the Scriptures might have hope." **(Romans 15:4)**

"And truly Jesus did many other signs in the presence of His disciples, which are not written in this book; but these are written that you may believe that Jesus is the Christ, the Son of God, and that believing you may have life in His name." **(John 20:30-31)**

In this chapter, we will be examining some selected miracles in the Old Testament and New Testament – ten in each of the Testaments – so you can understand better that every miracle you will ever need is already provided for by God. Please, pay attention to these wonders of God because at least one, if not all the miracles listed here will be manifested in your life before you are done reading this book and whenever you need it, in Jesus' name.

Of course, many of these miracles may be already known to you but I believe that there's something great the Lord wants to accomplish in your life as the miracles come alive in your mind again.

OLD TESTAMENT EXAMPLES

1. Glorious creation from nothingness

Hebrews 11:3 tells us that *"the universe was formed at God's command, so that what is seen was not made out of what was visible"* (NLT). This means that God practically created this whole universe, including the wondrous works of nature, out of nothing. Not only that, Genesis 1:1-2 reveals, *"In the beginning God created the heavens and the earth. The earth was without form, and void; and darkness was on the face of the deep. And the Spirit of God was hovering over the face of the waters"* (NKJV). When the earth was first created, it was empty, shapeless and full of darkness. Then something happened – the Spirit of God moved, and God spoke and everything began to take shape. Light, order and beauty replaced darkness, formlessness and emptiness. This is exactly what God is working out in your life too. You may currently think that your life is meaningless, empty, and hopeless, but I'm here to tell you that you are a work in progress; God is working something awesome, glorious, and outstanding out of you. When He is done, even you will be amazed at what He will make of you! The glory of God is about to break forth in your life. Your life is about to radiate God's beauty and glory permanently and perpetually, in Jesus' name.

2. Supernatural conception

Romans 4:16-20 (NKJV)

"Therefore it is of faith that it might be according to grace, so that the promise might be sure to all the seed, not only to those who are of the law, but also to those who are of the faith of Abraham, who is the father of us all (as it is written, "I have made you a father of many nations") in the presence of Him whom he believed—God, who gives life to the dead and calls those things which do not exist as though they did; who, contrary to hope, in hope believed, so that he became the father of many nations, according to what was spoken, "So shall your descendants be." And not being weak in faith, he did not consider his own body, already dead (since he was about a hundred years old), and the

deadness of Sarah's womb. He did not waver at the promise of God through unbelief, but was strengthened in faith, giving glory to God."

The conception and birth of Isaac totally defied natural and scientific explanations. According to Romans 4:16-20, both Abraham and Sarah were past the age of childbearing. In fact, the passage describes Abraham's body and Sarah's womb as being "dead". Yet the power of God injected life into their reproductive systems, when it was time for the child to be conceived.

It does not matter whatever report you may have received about your reproductive ability or chances of conception. I want to tell you that you are carrying a miracle baby, a seed of greatness is in you and you shall deliver that child in Jesus' name. From this moment, the power of God is penetrating your body and activating the process of successful conception and delivery, in Jesus' name.

3. Way out of nowhere

The crossing of the Red Sea is one of the most famous miracles in human history. The context within which it happened only helps to highlight its awesomeness. The Israelites found themselves "between the devil and the deep red sea." Closing in behind them were the furious and vicious armies of Egypt, bent on either recapturing them into captivity or totally wasting them. And right in front of them was the Red Sea that was naturally impassable.

It seemed all was over for God's people but then God showed Himself strong and mighty, as He always does. Before then, however, there was a declaration from Moses that you too can lay claim to today. Exodus 14:13-14 says, *"And Moses said unto the people, Fear ye not, stand still, and see the salvation of the LORD, which he will shew to you to day: for the Egyptians whom ye have seen to day, ye shall see them again no more for ever. The LORD shall fight for you, and ye shall hold your peace."* Thereafter, God instructed Moses to stretch his rod towards the sea and it parted for the Israelites to pass in their entirety, after which it closed up again to consume their advancing adversaries. What a miracle!

Whatever situation you may currently be in that makes it look like it's over for you, I assure you that God is making a way out of it right now!

4. From bitterness to sweetness

"Now when they came to Marah, they could not drink the waters of Marah, for they were bitter. Therefore the name of it was called Marah. And the people complained against Moses, saying, *"What shall we drink?"* So he cried *out to the Lord, and the Lord showed him a tree. When he cast it into the waters, the waters were made sweet"* Exodus 15:23-25 (NKJV).

Exodus 15:23-25 tells of how the Israelites needed water in the wilderness but unfortunately when they found some, it was bitter. Miraculously, however, God removed the bitterness by instructing Moses to cast a particular log of wood into it. Whatever it is that has been causing perpetual bitterness, sadness, sorrow and heartbreak in your life is transformed to sweetness from this moment, in Jesus' name. The Bible says that all things work together for the good of those who love God. Whatever it is that has been a source of sorrow to you is turning around to become a source of joy to you by the power of the Almighty God.

5.   Breakthrough from all limitations

As the Israelites neared the Promised Land of Canaan, they were to pass through the city of Jericho. However, the Bible reveals that *"Jericho was straitly shut up because of the children of Israel: none went out, and none came in."* (Joshua 6:1). Isn't this similar to the situation that confronts many people today? Despite their best efforts to reach their point of joy, success, achievement or fulfilment, there always seems to be a deliberate physical or spiritual barrier to frustrate their progress. I don't know whether this resonates with your situation, but

I'm here to let you know that the irresistible power of God will dismantle every barricade to your progress and breakthrough. Beginning from this moment, you will begin to make unhindered progress, in Jesus' name.

The Scripture says that the weapons of our welfare are not carnal but mighty through God for the pulling down of strongholds. Every stronghold that the enemy has constructed to prevent your progress in any area of life is being demolished by the power of God right now, in Jesus' name.

6. Extraordinary provision

There are indeed many miracles of divine provision in the Bible but I want to single out the case of Elijah at the brook of Cherith. This is because of the peculiarity of the instrument that God used. 1 Kings 17:2-6 says, *"And the word of the LORD came unto him, saying, Get thee hence, and turn thee eastward, and hide thyself by the brook Cherith, that is before Jordan. And it shall be, that thou shalt drink of the brook; and I have commanded the ravens to feed thee there. So he went and did according unto the word of the LORD: for he went and dwelt by the brook Cherith, that is before Jordan. And the ravens brought him bread and flesh in the morning, and bread and flesh in the evening; and he drank of the brook."*

If you know a thing or two about ravens, you will

appreciate the beauty of this miracle and the greatness of our God. Ravens are the least of birds that anyone could have imagined for such a task. This is partly because of their unreliable nature but mostly because they are indiscriminate devourers. Indeed, it is from this gluttonous nature of theirs that we have the word "ravenous". Yet, it was these same birds that it pleased God to use in bringing food to Elijah twice daily.

I decree into your life today that help, mercies and favors will come to you from people and places you least expect, in Jesus' name!

7. Gravity-defying restoration

Here again is an occurrence that science cannot explain. *"...And when they came to Jordan, they cut down wood. But as one was felling a beam, the axe head fell into the water: and he cried, and said, Alas, master! for it was borrowed. And the man of God said, Where fell it? And he shewed him the place. And he cut down a stick, and cast it in thither; and the iron did swim. Therefore said he, Take it up to thee. And he put out his hand, and took it."* (2 Kings 6:4-7).

Only God, with whom there is no impossibility, can make a metallic object that had sunk into the depths of a river to come floating back again. And it can happen in your life. Whatever good thing that has been lost in your life and you think can never be recovered, the Lord is recovering for you from this moment, in Jesus' name.

8. Promotion-triggering remembrance

Mordecai was due for promotion but no one seemed to remember this. Instead, they watched him linger in his lowly position, as almost a nonentity. In fact, Haman, his adversary, was plotting to make his life more miserable. But the Almighty God remembered him – as HE will remember you today – and what followed next was incredible. *"On that night could not the king sleep, and he commanded to bring the book of records of the chronicles; and they were read before the king. And it was found written, that Mordecai had told of Bigthana and Teresh, two of the king's chamberlains, the keepers of the door, who sought to lay hand on the king Ahasuerus. And the king said, What honour and dignity hath been done to Mordecai for this? Then said the king's servants that ministered unto him, There is nothing done for him."* (Esther 6:1-3).

If you read further in that book of Esther, you will discover that the previously forgotten and ignored Mordecai became the most honored and celebrated man in the kingdom. And not only that, the same Haman that was seeking his destruction became the "errand boy" that was announcing his exaltation around the kingdom. I declare that, beginning from this moment, you shall be remembered for promotion and exaltation in Jesus' name. All your God-appointed destiny-helpers and all who are supposed to approve your entitlements will no longer be able to rest until you get what God has purposed for you, in Jesus' name.

9. Wisdom and insights to provide unprecedented solutions

A great famine was to ravage the then world and the revelation came in form of two dreams to Pharaoh, who was about the most powerful ruler then. The problem was, nobody could unravel the meaning of the dreams and something told Pharaoh that there was something significant about those dreams. Sadly, not even the best magicians and astrologers that he had always relied upon could help him. Then someone recommended Joseph. And when the king presented the dreams to him, asking for the interpretations, Joseph plainly replied, *"It is not in me: God shall give Pharaoh an answer of peace."* (Genesis 41:16).

God, indeed, showed up for Joseph and the young man not only went ahead to accurately interpret the dreams but he also gave insightful recommendations on how to avert the looming doom. His suggestions were so remarkable and strategic that Pharaoh himself could not but exclaim, *"Can we find such a one as this is, a man in whom the Spirit of God is? And Pharaoh said unto Joseph,*

Forasmuch as God hath shewed thee all this, there is none so discreet and wise as thou art: Thou shalt be over my house, and according unto thy word shall all my people be ruled: only in the throne will I be greater than thou. And Pharaoh said unto Joseph, See, I have set thee over all the land of Egypt" (Genesis 41:38-41).

Joseph miraculously proved to be the solution-provider that the then world needed. I decree unto your life that the wisdom, insights, strategies and solutions to positively impact and transform your world will come on you, in the mighty name of Jesus.

10. Deliverance from conspirators and deadly snares

Jealousy and envy often stir up a bitter spirit that make people do desperate and, sometimes, deadly things. Such was the situation Daniel found himself in Babylon. As a result of the favors he enjoyed from the king – due to his diligence and faithfulness – some other officials began envying and plotting to eliminate him. They set up what they thought was a clever trap for him, which would inevitably lead him to being cast into a den of lions. Does this sound like what you are currently facing in your place of work, family or community?

Well, as it turned out, God intervened for Daniel by disrupting nature. Lions that are known to be ferocious and highly territorial carnivores suddenly lost appetite for flesh and only saw Daniel as being uneatable. As the Bible says in John 1:5, *"The light shines in the darkness, and the darkness can never extinguish it."* (NLT). I declare you uneatable, untouchable, unstoppable, unconquerable, and inextinguishable to your enemies, in the name of Jesus.

To show that it was God who intervened on Daniel's behalf and not that the lions were sick or had become vegetarians, the Bible says that when it became clear to the king that there was indeed a conspiracy against Daniel, he triggered a boomerang. *"So Daniel was taken up out of the den, and no manner of hurt was found upon him, because he believed in his God. And the king commanded, and they brought those men which had accused Daniel, and they cast them into the den of lions, them, their children, and their wives; and the lions had the mastery of them, and brake all their bones in pieces or ever they came at the bottom of the den"* (Daniel 6:23-24). In the name that is above every name, every negative fire set up by the enemy to burn you and anyone in your family, they, themselves shall fall into it, in Jesus' name.

NEW TESTAMENT EXAMPLES

1. Mistake turned to a miracle

If you can recall, the first miracle that Jesus performed was at a wedding at Cana, in Galilee, and there is a message of hope and assurance for you in it. The organizers of that wedding had made a major mistake in planning for it – they had not arranged for enough wine. Thus, when it was time for entertainment, the wine got finished. As wine-drinking was a key part of their ceremonies then, there was a lot of panic among the organizers. What had begun as a joyous ceremony was about to end in embarrassment. Just then, Jesus was consulted and a spectacular twist was introduced to the event - such that what was to become a source of disgrace became a source of wonder to everyone present. *"Jesus saith unto them, Fill the waterpots with water. And they filled them up to the brim. And he saith unto them, Draw out now, and bear unto the governor of the feast. And they bare it. When the ruler of the feast had tasted the water that was made wine, and knew not whence it was: (but the servants which drew the water knew;) the governor of the feast called the bridegroom, And saith unto him, Every man at the beginning doth set forth good wine; and when men have well drunk, then that which is worse: but thou hast kept the good wine until now."* (John 2:7-10).

What mistake have you or your parents made in the past – especially before your coming to know Christ – and you think it will continually be a source of stigma, shame, and limitation to your destiny? Cheer up, child of God, and hand it over to God. That blunder will become an uncommon blessing to your life. It shall be to you a miracle which the world we join you to glorify God for.

2. Success in a previous area of failure

When Jesus met Peter and the other disciples at the Lake of Gennesaret, they were at the point of frustration. According to Peter, *"We have toiled all night and caught nothing"* (Luke 5:5). However, as soon as Jesus showed up and gave a command for them to launch into the deep again, we are told that *"they caught a great number of fish, and their net was breaking. So they signaled to their partners in the other boat to come and help them. And they came and filled both the boats, so that they began to sink."* (Luke 5:6-7). In essence, they recorded a huge success at that same place that they had recorded repeated failure. Wherever it is that you have failed in the past; whatever it is that you have tried and tried and failed at, I declare that from now, you will begin to succeed in such areas, in Jesus' name.

3. Protection from accident and aborted destiny

What was meant to be a simple journey was almost hijacked by the forces of nature and perhaps the forces of darkness with the aim of turning it to a tale of calamity and lamentations. At the instruction of Jesus Christ Himself, the disciples had set out on a journey across the sea. Not even in the wildest of imagination of the disciples, most of whom used to be expert fishermen – could they have imagined the ferocity of the storm that arose against them. So fearsome was it that they thought their lives were over because their boat seemed to be getting swamped. In panic, they ran to Jesus, who was resting peacefully, and He wondered how they could imagine that their boat would capsize while he was there with them. He arose, silenced the storm and not only was calmness restored but the Bible affirms that they successfully *"came over unto the other side."* (Mark 4:35-41; 5:1). The question is – is Jesus in the boat of your life? He is the miracle worker; bring Him into the boat of your life today, and you will experience eternal miracles.

I declare unto your life that accident will not claim your life or that of your loved ones. I decree that whatever storm may arise, your life and destiny will not be cut short, in Jesus' name.

4. Deliverance from demonic oppressions and mental disorders

Perhaps, one of the reasons the great storm arose against Jesus and His disciples in Mark 4 was because the time of deliverance had come for the possessed man of Gadara, who was on the other side. This man had become so demonically possessed and mentally deranged that he was no longer living among humans. Of all places anyone could think of, he chose to live in the graveyard. Simply put, his destiny had been turned upside down. But just one encounter with Jesus brought him back to sanity and consequently restored him to his rightly place in destiny. *"And they come to Jesus, and see him that was possessed with the devil, and had the legion, sitting, and clothed, and in his right mind…"* (Mark 5:15).

Whatever it is that has taken over your mind or life, causing endless depression and affliction; whatever it is that makes you suicidal or confines you to where you do not belong is being lifted out of your life now by the omnipotent power of the Most High God, in Jesus mighty name.

5.   Deliverance from ruinous addictions

Many people indulge in self-destructive behavior, not because they enjoy what they are doing but because they are not in control of their lives. Many children and youths seem out of control, not because they are happy to be causing their parents sorrow but because their lives are helplessly taken over by satanic influences.

Such was the case of the child that was brought to Jesus in Mark 9. *"And one of the multitude answered and said, Master, I have brought unto thee my son, which hath a dumb spirit; And wheresoever he taketh him, he teareth him: and he foameth, and gnasheth with his teeth, and pineth away... And ofttimes it hath cast him into the fire, and into the waters, to destroy him: but if thou canst do any thing, have compassion on us, and help us... When Jesus saw that the people came running together, he rebuked the foul spirit, saying unto him, Thou dumb and deaf spirit, I charge thee, come out of him, and enter no more into him. And the spirit cried, and rent him sore, and came out of him: and he was as one dead; insomuch that many said, He is dead. But Jesus took him by the hand, and lifted him up; and he arose."* (Mark 9:17-27).

Maybe this describes you or anyone around you. The liberating power of Jesus Christ is available to break every chain of addiction and ruinous behavior in your life and family.

6.   Healing for incurable disease

The woman with the issue of blood is described as one who had suffered so much, not only because her disease had stayed for 12 years but also because she had suffered a lot of shame and lost a lot of money, without any hope of ever finding a cure. Doctors had done all they could but there seemed to be no cure. But, of course, with Jesus, there are no incurable diseases or hopeless cases. Just one touch of Jesus' garment by the woman and we are told that *"immediately her flow of blood stopped."* (Luke 8:44).

Under the authority of the Lord Jesus Christ, I speak to the fountain of any and all incurable diseases in your life to begin to dry up from this moment in Jesus' mighty name. As from today, you shall no longer live in sickness or disease, in Jesus' name.

7. The Miracle of Multiplication

Matthew 14:17-21 (NKJV)

And they said to Him, *"We have here only five loaves and two fish."* He said, *"Bring them here to Me."* Then He commanded the multitudes to sit down on the grass. And He took the five loaves and the two fish, and looking up to heaven, He blessed and broke and gave the loaves to the disciples; and the disciples gave to the multitudes. So they all ate and were filled, and they took up twelve baskets full of the fragments that remained. Now those who had eaten were about five thousand men, besides women and children.

As recorded in the Gospels, it was only five loaves of bread and two fishes surrendered by a little boy that Jesus was able to feed over 5000 people, and there were twelve baskets of leftovers. Whatever God has told you to do with your talent and gift, or whatever venture He has instructed you to begin, go ahead and do it. The anointing for exponential increase and multiplication will come on that investment and it flourish beyond your wildest imagination. I decree that your "little light" will shine across nations and generations in the name of Jesus.

8. History-making strides

Until Jesus empowered Peter to miraculously join Him to walk on water, nobody else in his family, community or nation had ever done so (Matthew 14:22-33). Indeed, no one in history had ever done it. But Peter did. My prayer for you today is that by the miraculous and empowering power of the Almighty God. You will do what no one has ever done in your family, organization, community and nation. You will discover what no one has discovered before and become a history-maker in the name of Jesus.

9. Unexpected divine visitation

As the lame man at the gate called beautiful fixed his eyes on Peter and John, all he expected was just to be given a few coins as alms; he probably had never experienced a major miracle in his life. He had simply accepted his fate; but God rejected that fate for him. *"And Peter, fastening his eyes upon him with John, said, Look on us. And he gave heed unto them, expecting to receive something of them. Then Peter said, Silver and gold have I none; but such as I have give I thee: In the name of Jesus Christ of*

Nazareth rise up and walk. And he took him by the right hand, and lifted him up: and immediately his feet and ankle bones received strength. " (Acts 3:4-7)

I pray that God will overturn every negative "fate" and declaration upon your life. I decree that you will receive a miracle that you never imagine could happen in Jesus' precious name.

10. Deliverance from captivity and stagnation

For doing the works of the Kingdom, Paul and Silas were arrested, beaten, chained and confined to prison. But the power of God shook the foundations of prison, shattered the chains of His children and unlocked the doors of the prison for them to regain their freedom.

"But at midnight Paul and Silas were praying and singing hymns to God, and the prisoners were listening to them. 26 Suddenly there was a great earthquake, so that the foundations of the prison were shaken; and immediately all the doors were opened and everyone's chains were loosed" (Acts 16:25-26 NKJV)

You cannot and should not be bound as a child of God. If you feel in any way bound, confined, stagnated or unfulfilled, it is not the will of God for you and His power is available to set you totally free.

Of course, there are still several more miracles in God's word for your benefit but it is not really about knowing these miracles but seeing them become realities in your life. How can this be achieved? Let's begin the process from the next chapter.

4

OPERATING IN THE MIRACULOUS

"Seeing a miracle will inspire you, but knowing you are a miracle will change you." – **Deborah Brodie**

"Most assuredly, I say to you, he who believes in Me, the works that I do he will do also; and greater works than these he will do, because I go to My Father. **(John 14:12)**

"And these signs will follow those who believe: In My name they will cast out demons; they will speak with new tongues; they will take up serpents; and if they drink anything deadly, it will by no means hurt them; they will lay hands on the sick, and they will recover." **(Mark 16:17-18)**

All that we have unraveled in the preceding chapters point to one truth: It is a pleasant and blessed experience to receive a miracle. However, God's greatest desire for you is that you live and operate in the miraculous. A miracle, as we have seen, is a manifestation of God's supernatural power and abilities. And we have already seen several examples of such manifestations. However, to demonstrate or dispense this power, as a believer, either to meet your own need or the need of others, or simply to advance God's Kingdom, is to operate in the miraculous.

Operating in the miraculous therefore means acting as God's instrument of ministering abundant life to ourselves and to the world (John 10:10); it is to be His *"sharp threshing instrument"* that will *"thresh the mountains, and beat them small"* (Isaiah 41:15). It is to function as God's vessel for exercising dominion over the works of the devil and everything that opposes the will and purpose of God.

God intends and expects operating in the miraculous to be the natural and daily experience of every believer in Christ - regardless of gender, age or position in the church. Jesus made this clear in Mark 16:17-18, where He says, *"And these signs shall follow them that believe; In my name shall they cast out devils; they shall speak with new tongues; They shall take up serpents; and if they drink any deadly thing, it shall not hurt them; they shall lay hands on the sick, and they shall recover."*

We have previously established that miracles are sometimes described as "signs" in the Bible. And you have to understand that the original Greek word translated into "signs" in the above passage and throughout the New Testament is the word *semeion*. This was the word used in describing the signature or seal of authenticity of a document. It was also used to describe the official written notice for announcing the final verdict of a court.

When you apply this in the context in which Christ uttered the above words, you would realize that He was simply saying that operating in the miraculous is God's uniform and badge for the believer. It is so fundamental to our living the Christian life that the absence of it could make our faith questionable.

Then there is also the word "follow". In the original Greek text, this word comes a powerful combination of two words – *para* and *akoloutheo* to form *paraakoloutheo*. I called this a powerful combo because on its own, *para* means "alongside", as in "side-by-side"; while *akoloutheo* means "to accompany" or "to travel with". Hallelujah! This means that God expects you and me to be so enveloped in His miracle-working power that it naturally and effortlessly oozes out of us all the time and anywhere!

RECOGNIZING YOUR DIVINE IDENTITY AND POSITIONING

To better understand why operating in the miraculous is such a big deal to God, we have to recognize who we truly are as heirs of God's Kingdom and the position of authority we occupy on earth. The Bible says that *"as many as received him, to them gave he power to become the sons of God, even to them that believe on his name."* (John 1:12). Being children of God means having the DNA of God and therefore behaving and functioning like Him. As a believer, you are more than an "ordinary" human being; you are a spiritual being, with supernatural capabilities for extraordinary possibilities!

A lion never births a donkey or even a cub that behaves like a donkey. As early as just two years old, a lion cub has mastered the art of roaring against enemies, together with almost all the hunting skills it needs to survive and dominate the animal kingdom. I don't know how old you are in Christ and it really doesn't matter, but by reason of your identity as a child of God, you must know that since God is a miracle-worker, you also are a miracle-worker. You are, by default, a carrier of God's miracle-power! You are one of His representatives on earth, and letting His power flow in and through you is one of the reasons He has brought you into His Kingdom in the first place! *"This people have I formed for myself; they shall shew forth my praise."* (Isaiah 43:21).

Still on our identity and positioning, Ephesians 2:4-6 says, *"But God, who is rich in mercy, for his great love wherewith he loved us, even when we were dead in sins, hath quickened us together with Christ, (by grace ye are saved;) And hath raised us up together, and made us sit together in heavenly places in Christ Jesus."* Sitting together with Jesus Christ in the heavenly places positions you in the same realm of authority from which He operated while on earth. This realm of authority, according to Ephesians 1:21, is such that is *"far above all principality, and power, and might, and dominion, and every name that is named, not only in this world, but also in that which is to come."*

It was for this reason that no crisis, sickness, disease, demon, enchantment, divination, manipulation or satanic attack could withstand the authority of Jesus Christ. And if you are truly seated with Him in the same place by redemption, this is how your life should be operating. Jesus Himself affirmed this, when He said, *"Verily, verily, I say unto you, He that believeth on me, the works that I do shall he do also; and greater works than these shall he do; because I go unto my Father."* (John 14:12). Isn't this so mightily empowering!

If you are familiar with the life of Jesus Christ, you would agree that He did many mighty works, so many that not all could be recorded. Those who were close to Him while on earth testified that He *"went about doing good, and healing all that were oppressed of the devil; for God was with him."* (Acts 10:38). Now, imagine the same Jesus Christ saying that not only are you supposed to be doing same things that He did but actually going far beyond because while He lived for just about 33 years before returning to the Father, you still have many more years to live on earth. This is what it means to function in the miraculous!

In case you still need additional proof of the exalted place you occupy as a believer, which makes it fundamental that you operate in the miraculous, I will show you something before moving to another vital recognition you must make. Romans 8:29 reveals, *"For whom he did foreknow, he also did predestinate to be conformed to the image of his Son, that he might be the firstborn among many brethren."*

I believe the picture of your identity should be much clearer to you now. As a born-again child of God, you were saved to be conformed to the image of Christ, such that you become a "mini-Christ" yourself. Jesus Christ thus becomes your Older Brother, while you are His identical younger brother – living the same life and exercising the same authority and dominion as He did.

It was this resemblance that the people of Antioch saw that made them to call the disciples "Christians" (mini-Christs) in the first place (Acts 11:26). Particularly for

Peter and John, who were initially known to be lowly fishermen, they so much lived in this realm of dominion in which Christ lived that people could not help noticing that they shared the same DNA with Jesus. Acts 4:13 says, *"Now when they saw the boldness of Peter and John, and perceived that they were unlearned and ignorant men, they marveled; and they took knowledge of them, that they had been with Jesus."*

This is the life that you have been called to live too – a life that boldly and victoriously confronts sin, sickness, Satan and every work of darkness; a life that radiates and dispenses miracles that make people marvel at the greatness and omnipotence of God!

RECOGNIZING YOUR DIVINE PRIVILEGES AND PROVISIONS

It will further galvanize you towards operating in the miraculous when you realize the privileges and provisions that have been made for you as a *bona fide* member of God's family and Kingdom. 2 Peter 1:3-4 says, *"According as his divine power hath given unto us all things that pertain unto life and godliness, through the knowledge of him that hath called us to glory and virtue: Whereby are given unto us exceeding great and precious promises: that by these ye might be partakers of the divine nature..."*

You already have all you need to be a partaker and transmitter of God's nature and miracle-working power. The birth, death and resurrection of Jesus Christ have accomplished all that you need to daily experience and dispense miracles. In other words, this is not something you have to struggle to bring to manifestation; it is something that is already there, which you just have to appropriate and leverage to the glory of God's name.

To start with, the Scripture says that "for this purpose the Son of God was manifested to destroy the works of the devil." Most of the afflictions and limitations that plague mankind are orchestrated by the devil and his demonic forces. But here the Scriptures make it clear that the works of the devil on earth have been destroyed by Jesus Christ in the spiritual realm. All that we do as believers and transmitters of God's miracle power is bringing this victory to physical manifestation in our lives and in the world, as a whole.

Still on the privileges and provisions that we have in Christ, as believers, the Bible says, *"Blotting out the handwriting of ordinances that was against us, which was contrary to us, and took it out of the way, nailing it to his cross; And having spoiled principalities and powers, he made a shew of them openly, triumphing over them in it."* (Colossians 2:14-15). Here, again, is a reminder that whatever factors or forces that should have hindered your ability to operate in God's supernatural power have been blotted out and neutralized by the power of the cross. Therefore, as one who has been redeemed by the blood of Jesus Christ, you can stand in the provisions and accomplishments of the cross to call forth the will of God to be established on the earth.

Additionally, Galatians 3:13-14 assures us that *"Christ hath redeemed us from the curse of the law, being made a curse for us: for it is written, Cursed is every one that hangeth on a tree: That the blessing of Abraham might come on the Gentiles through Jesus Christ; that we might receive the promise of the Spirit through faith."* Did you see that? Jesus has done the work for you and me already. He has taken off the curse of limitations from us and opened the doorway to the blessing of Abraham for you and the rest of humanity to enjoy. This blessing of Abraham is aptly summarized in Genesis 24:1 thus: *"Now Abraham was old, well advanced in age; and the LORD had blessed Abraham in all things"* (NKJV). This is the kind of life that Christ has given you the access to enjoy by His victory on the cross. When you realize that the price is paid for you to enjoy all-round blessings, then you cannot but reject and cancel anything that makes you or others live a substandard life.

To further emphasize how privileged and well-provided-for we are, as believers, the Scripture reminds us that

Jesus Christ was "wounded for our transgressions, he was bruised for our iniquities: the chastisement of our peace was upon him; and with his stripes we are healed." (Isaiah 53:5). All we need to enjoy total forgiveness and freedom from sin; all we need to enjoy peace that passes all understanding; and all we need to enjoy healing and good health have been provided in Christ Jesus. 2 Corinthians 8:9 equally adds that *"For you know the grace of our Lord Jesus Christ, that though he was rich, yet for your sake he became poor, so that you through his poverty might become rich."*

With all of these provisions and many more, you can understand why God cannot but expect your life to be a prolific powerhouse of miracles. In fact, it was in view of all this that Jesus, having borne and endured all He needed to endure to accomplish our all-round victory, declared, as He was about dying on the cross – IT IS FINISHED! Yes, it is done. Everything you need to be a living and mobile miracle is available!

FUNCTIONING WITH YOUR DIVINE ANOINTING AND AUTHORITY

The climax of the "why" you are expected to operate in the miraculous is the power and authority that God has conferred upon you, as a believer. In Luke 10:19, Jesus says, *"Behold, I give unto you power to tread on serpents and scorpions, and over all the power of the enemy: and nothing shall by any means hurt you."* What a glorious and thunderous power you carry as a believer! Serpents and scorpions represent the forces and situations that inject sorrow, sadness, distress, weakness, helplessness and hopelessness into people's lives. And Jesus says that you have the power to crush such destructive and debilitating agents wherever they manifest.

Interestingly, as it often happens today, even the disciples of Jesus did not initially understand the enormity of the power that they carried within them. Jesus, therefore, had to give them a practical demonstration. *"And on the morrow, when they were come from Bethany, he was hungry: And seeing a fig tree afar off having leaves, he came, if haply he might find any thing thereon: and when he came to it, he found nothing but leaves; for the time of figs was not yet. And Jesus answered and said unto it, No man eat fruit of thee hereafter for ever. And his disciples heard it…And in the morning, as they passed by, they saw the fig tree dried up from the roots. And Peter calling to remembrance saith unto him, Master, behold, the fig tree which thou cursedst is withered away. And Jesus answering saith unto them, Have faith in God. For verily I say unto you, That whosoever shall say unto this mountain, Be thou removed, and be thou cast into the sea; and shall not doubt in his heart, but shall believe that those things which he saith shall come to pass; he shall have whatsoever he saith. Therefore I say unto you, What things soever ye desire, when ye pray, believe that ye receive them, and ye shall have them."* (Mark 11:12-24).

While the disciples were still marveling at the withering of the fig tree, in response the declaration of Jesus, He told them plainly that they could do even much more. It was a tree that He eliminated; they could, in fact, eliminate MOUNTAINS! This is the power and the authority that God has deposited in us as His children. Like Jeremiah, we have been called and empowered *"to root out and to pull down, to destroy and to throw down, to build and to plant"* – according to the power of God that works within us.

ALIGNING WITH GOD'S GREAT ARMY OF MIRACLE-WORKERS

Now, as a proof that operating in the miraculous and doing "greater works" can become a routine part of our lives, we have examples of men and women in the Bible and in our day who have demonstrated this possibility. In fact, the Bible specifically calls our attention to someone like Elijah, saying: *"Elijah was as human as we are, and yet when he prayed earnestly that no rain would fall, none fell for three and a half years! Then, when he prayed again, the sky sent down rain and the earth began to yield its crops."* (James 5:17-18, NLT).

Saying "Elijah was as human as we are" is another way

of saying there is nothing Elijah did that you cannot do as a believer today. Joshua 10:12-13 also gives us the example of Joshua: *"Then spake Joshua to the LORD in the day when the LORD delivered up the Amorites before the children of Israel, and he said in the sight of Israel, Sun, stand thou still upon Gibeon; and thou, Moon, in the valley of Ajalon. And the sun stood still, and the moon stayed, until the people had avenged themselves upon their enemies…"*

You can imagine how people who lived under the dispensation of the law – when Christ had not died and resurrected – operated in the miraculous. How much more should we, under the dispensation of grace and the Holy Spirit, operate!

The apostles of Jesus, indeed, showed us that our time is such that should witness greater manifestations of the miraculous through us. These demonstrations began while Jesus was still physically with them, and after He went to heaven, they continued with the ministrations. I have shown you how Peter and John dispensed healing and deliverance to the cripple at the temple gate. I have also shown you how Paul and Silas shattered prison chains and unlocked closed doors. But there is so much more that happened that cannot be recounted here. The Bible, in summarizing these, says: *"many signs and wonders were regularly done among the people by the hands of the apostles"* (Acts 5:12, ESV). This means that operating in the miraculous had become a way of life for them.

Indeed, in line with Jesus' prediction of "greater works", things got so intense with the apostles, *"Insomuch that they brought forth the sick into the streets, and laid them on beds and couches, that at the least the shadow of Peter passing by might overshadow some of them. There came also a multitude out of the cities round about unto Jerusalem, bringing sick folks, and them which were vexed with unclean spirits: and they were healed every one."* (Acts 5:15-16). It is similarly reported in Acts 19:11-12 that *"God wrought special miracles by the hands of Paul: So that from his body were brought unto the sick handkerchiefs or aprons, and the diseases departed from them, and the evil spirits went out of them."*

This, again, is what it means to operate in the miraculous and it is the life that God has called and equipped you to live. The reasons for this, from all we have seen in this chapter, are apparent. One, it is by operating in the miraculous that you can exercise and enjoy full dominion on earth as a child of God. Without being able to operate in the miraculous anyone would live a limited life and easily become a plaything to the devil. It is by operating in the miraculous that you can fully actualize the plans of God for your life, while neutralizing every manifestation of the works of the devil. Two, as we have seen already, this is a major way to affirm the validity of your identity and ministry as God's child. When the serpent that attacked Paul on the Island of Malta could not hurt him, contrary to the expectations of the people, they could not help recognizing and declaring that he was a supernatural being (Acts 28:3-6).

Three, it is by operating in the miraculous that you can fulfil your mandate as the salt and light of the world (Matthew 5:13-16). Salt sweetens and light banishes darkness. We cannot fully bring gladness to people's lives, without being able to banish the works of darkness that trouble them. It is said in Acts 8:8 that there was great joy in Samaria. Why? *"For unclean spirits, crying with loud voice, came out of many that were possessed with them: and many taken with palsies, and that were lame, were healed"* (Acts 8:7). Earlier on, Jesus had emphasized that operating in the miraculous was a crucial part of His ministry of bringing joy and hope to humanity. He declared, *"The Spirit of the Lord is upon me, because he hath anointed me to preach the gospel to the poor; he hath sent me to heal the brokenhearted, to preach deliverance to the captives, and recovering of sight to the blind, to set at liberty them that are bruised, To preach the acceptable year of the Lord."* (Luke 4:18-19). We cannot claim to be proclaiming "Good News" while we or the people we are ministering to remain helplessly bound by the works of the devil.

Four, operating in the miraculous is one of the surest ways to demonstrate the supremacy of God and draw people to His kingdom. In Acts 8 that we referenced earlier about the ministry of Philip, the Bible adds that *"the people with one accord gave heed unto those things which Philip spake, hearing and seeing the miracles which he did."* (Acts 8:6). Jesus Christ was particularly fond of advertising the gospel with miracles. He often healed and delivered people who needed divine intervention in their situations, which usually resulted in more people trooping out to hear Him preach (Matthew 4:23-25).

Five, it provides a strong immunity against the deceptions and snares of satanic agents, who disguise themselves as miracle-workers. Ignorance and incapability to operate in the miraculous have made many believers to not only perpetually remain in bondage but to also become prey to false miracle-workers. It is baffling and depressing to read and hear stories of the horrible and demeaning things that these satanic agents subject make some supposed children of God to in the name of "deliverance".

Last but not the least, operating in the miraculous is a guaranteed way to enforce God's will on earth, as well as advance His kingdom. *"And from the days of John the Baptist until now the kingdom of heaven suffereth violence, and the violent take it by force."* (Matthew 11:12).

Let us proceed to see the steps to making this a reality!

5

KEYS TO OPERATING IN THE MIRACULOUS

"Our God is a miracle-working God! He still steps in to heal, to answer prayer, to perform His purposes." - **John Napier**

"For assuredly, I say to you, whoever says to this mountain, 'Be removed and be cast into the sea,' and does not doubt in his heart, but believes that those things he says will be done, he will have whatever he says. Therefore I say to you, whatever things you ask when you pray, believe that you receive them, and you will have them." **(Matthew 11:23-24).**

"Elijah was a man with a nature like ours, and he prayed earnestly that it would not rain; and it did not rain on the land for three years and six months. 18 And he prayed again, and the heaven gave rain, and the earth produced its fruit." **(James 5:17-18)**

We have now come much closer to the crux of our exposition on the miraculous. So much have we learned about miracles and the miraculous life. We have realized, among several other truths, that God does not want us to perpetually remain at the level of being spoon-fed with miracles by others; rather, He wants us to advance to the level of activating and dispensing miracles for the benefit of ourselves and others. This is the realm of the miraculous.

Therefore, the most pertinent question now is, how exactly do we access the realm of the miraculous? How do we live the daily life of uncommon and unstoppable power, victory, dominion and impact that God has ordained and mandated for us? The quick answer to this is for us to get the master key that automatically and unfailingly opens the door to the miraculous. This key works anywhere and anytime! Indeed, every genuine miracle that occurs is traceable to this master key. Likewise, every miracle that endures the tests of time has its root in it. This is why I call it the "Master Key" or "the assured pathway" to the miraculous.

You may be wondering what this master key or assured pathway is and why it is called so. We will come to this later but first we must answer a more pressing question. Does mentioning a master key or an "assured" pathway mean that there are other keys and pathways? Certainly!

What does a key do? It opens. Therefore, since there are other keys that also open the door to the miraculous, we must give them some attention before proceeding to dwell on the master key and show why it is the preeminent key for unlocking miracles!

KEY ONE: PRAYER

Throughout the history of mankind, prayer has been a powerful pathway for attracting divine attention and blessings. Countless miracles have been obtained and multitudes of lives, destinies and situations have been changed by the power of prayer. The Bible, on various occasions, actually enjoins us to make prayer a lifestyle, not just because it is the easiest way we can directly communicate with God but also because it is mightily potent in operating in the miraculous. James 5:16 declares that *"the effectual fervent prayer of a righteous man availeth much"* and proceeds to cite the example of Elijah who used prayers to lock and later unlock the windows of heaven to influence rainfall in Israel.

Samuel Chadwick once said of prayer that it "turns ordinary mortals into men of power. It brings power. It brings fire. It brings rain. It brings life. It brings God." Andy Murray too adds that "prayer opens the way for God Himself to do His work in us and through us." Indeed time and space will not allow us to recount the numerous examples of people we know in the Bible and in our present time who mightily operated in the miraculous through the key and pathway of prayer. Prominently, though, we know of Isaac, who prayed for his wife to conceive and she did. We know of Jacob, who prayed all night long and both his name and destiny were changed. We know of Jabez, who despite being given an accursed name from birth, went on to become "more honorable" through the power of prayer.

We also know of Hannah, whose heartfelt prayer in Shiloh, led to the birth of Samuel (1 Samuel 1:10-20). We know of David who prayed that God would confound the counsel of Ahitophel and it happened. We know of Elijah who called down fire from heaven by fire (1 Kings 18:36-38). We know of Hezekiah, who reversed the pronouncement of death on him and consequently extended his lifespan (2 Kings 20:1-7). We know of Asa who prayed and the enemies were crushed (2 Chronicles 14:11-15). In the New Testament, we know that Jesus Christ prayed on several occasions and got results. Similarly, the apostles prayed many times and miracles happened. In particular, we know of how when Peter was imprisoned and was to be killed by Herod, the church prayed and he was miraculously rescued.

However, as effective as prayer is, it is not the master key to the miraculous. You know why? It is not all prayers - even from believers – that get answered. This is because of our natural tendency to pray amiss - perhaps out of ignorance, self-centeredness, self-will, carnality or sheer vanity. Apostle James explained this to the recipients of his epistle: *"From whence come wars and fightings among you? come they not hence, even of your lusts that war in your members? Ye lust, and have not: ye kill, and desire to have, and cannot obtain: ye fight and war, yet ye have not, because ye ask not. Ye ask, and receive not, because ye ask amiss, that ye may consume it upon your lusts."* (James 4:1-3). Providing further insight on this, Philip Graham Ryken wrote: *"Our trouble is that so often we come to God with our greeds rather than our needs... This becomes the source of our discontent: we desire things that God has not promised."*

Sometimes, though, the problem is not from our human failings but from the limitations of our natural language. This is why the Bible says, *"likewise the Spirit also helpeth our infirmities: for we know not what we should pray for as we ought: but the Spirit itself maketh intercession for us with groanings which cannot be uttered."* (Romans 8:26).

The case of King David shows us that not all prayers bring result, and that even the best of believers can pray amiss. *"...And the LORD struck the child that Uriah's wife bare unto David, and he was very sick. David therefore besought God for the child; and David fasted, and went in, and lay all night upon the earth. And the elders of his house arose, and went to him, to raise him up from the earth: but he would not, neither did he eat bread with them. And it came to pass on the seventh day, that the child died."* (2 Samuel 12:15-18).

God did not answer David's prayer, even though he added fasting and crying, and did not stop for many days. The reason is because his prayer was contrary to God's will. It was emotion-driven. Sadly, even though God is compassionate, He cannot be swayed by emotions; what moves Him is the master key, which will be unraveled shortly.

KEY 2: PRAISE

God loves to be praised, and praising Him works wonders. In fact, the Bible says that God is *"fearful in praises, doing wonders."* (Exodus 15:11). Psalm 100:3-4 is even more direct in saying that praise is a key to accessing God's presence for blessings. *"Know ye that the LORD he is God: it is he that hath made us, and not we ourselves; we are his people, and the sheep of his pasture. Enter into his gates with thanksgiving, and into his courts with praise: be thankful unto him, and bless his name."*

Many mountains and burdens that had refused to budge in the face of prayer had crashed before the sounds of praise. John Livingstone, attesting to this, said: *"Oh, how fully I am persuaded that a line of praises is worth a leaf [page] of prayer, and an hour of praises is worth a day of fasting and mourning."*

Earlier on, we have seen proofs of the power of praise in the mighty miracle that Paul and Silas received in prison. *"And at midnight Paul and Silas prayed, and sang praises unto God: and the prisoners heard them. And suddenly there was a great earthquake, so that the foundations of the prison were shaken: and immediately all the doors were opened, and every one's bands were loosed."* (Acts 16:25-26).

Much earlier, in the Old Testament, there is an amazing account of how the people of Judah, led by Jehoshaphat, successfully defeated the three nations that had combined to wage a vicious war against them: *"And they rose early in the morning, and went forth into the wilderness of Tekoa: and as they went forth, Jehoshaphat stood and said, Hear me, O Judah, and ye inhabitants of Jerusalem; Believe in the LORD your God, so shall ye be established; believe his prophets, so shall ye prosper. And when he had consulted with the people, he appointed singers unto the LORD, and that should praise the beauty of holiness, as they went out before the army, and to say, Praise the LORD; for his mercy endureth for ever. And when they began to sing and to praise, the LORD set ambushments against the children of*

71

Ammon, Moab, and mount Seir, which were come against Judah; and they were smitten. " (2 Chronicles 20:20-22).

There are other examples of such victories obtained by God's people in Bible times through praises. In our contemporary time, the testimony is the same. It is said, for example, that the people of Feldkirch, in Austria, were able to escape the threats of invasion by the army of Napoleon Buonaparte by simply worshipping God. As the narrative goes, at first, the people were troubled and confused about what to do. Napoleon's army was massive and known to be ruthless. Soldiers had been spotted on the heights above the little town, which was situated on the Austrian border. A council of citizens was hastily summoned to decide whether they should try to defend themselves or display the white flag of surrender.

Fortunately, the day was Easter Sunday, and the people had gathered in the local church. The pastor rose and said, "Friends, we have been counting on our own strength, and apparently that has failed. As this is the day of our Lord's resurrection, let us just ring the bells to worship God, and leave the matter in His hands. We know only our weakness, and not the power of God to defend us."

The council accepted his plan and the church bells rang. The enemy, hearing the sudden peal, concluded that the

Austrian army had arrived during the night to defend the town. Before the service ended, the enemy broke camp and left.

There are other testimonies I can share, even from my own life. Notwithstanding, just like prayer, praise is not the master key to the miraculous because it can also be done amiss and can actually be repulsive to God. As Matthew 15:8 says, "This people draweth nigh unto me with their mouth, and honoureth me with their lips; but their heart is far from me." This is even more pronounced in present day when the line between spiritual praise and worship to God and mere fleshly entertainment has become increasingly blurry in many congregations.

KEY 3: GIVING

Historically, giving has always been a tested and trusted door-opener and miracle-propeller. This is apparently due to its strong connection with the natural law of sowing and reaping. So powerful is the key of giving that Christ Himself taught that *"It is more blessed to give than to receive"* (Acts 20:35). There are many other instances where the Bible enjoins us to give, with the expectation of overflowing returns (see, for example, Luke 6:38; Malachi 3:10; Proverbs 3:9-10; 19:17).

Specifically for unleashing the miraculous, giving is so powerful that it can lead to a miracle, even if you don't seek one. You would easily understand what this means if you can recall the link to the law of sowing and reaping, as previously noted. Sometimes an individual unconsciously drops a seed into the ground, without giving it much thought, until the seed begins to germinate into a viable plant and eventually producing fruits.

A clear example of how giving can lead to unexpected breakthrough is contained in 2 Kings 4:8-36: *"And it fell on a day, that Elisha passed to Shunem, where was a great woman; and she constrained him to eat bread. And so it was, that as oft as he passed by, he turned in thither to eat bread. And she said unto her husband, Behold now, I perceive that this is an holy man of God, which passeth by us continually. Let us make a little chamber, I pray thee, on the wall; and let us set for him there a bed, and a table, and a stool, and a candlestick: and it shall be, when he cometh to us, that he shall turn in thither. And it fell on a day, that he came thither, and he turned into the chamber, and lay there. And he said to Gehazi his servant, Call this Shunammite. And when he had called her, she stood before him. And he said unto him, Say now unto her, Behold, thou hast been careful for us with all this care; what is to be done for thee? wouldest thou be spoken for to the king, or to the captain of the host? And she answered, I dwell among mine own people. And he said, What then is to be done for her? And Gehazi answered, Verily she hath no child, and her husband is old. And he said, Call her. And when he had called her, she stood in the door. And he said, About this season, according to the time of life, thou shalt embrace a son. And she said, Nay, my lord, thou man of God, do not lie unto thine handmaid. And the woman conceived, and bare a son at that season that Elisha had said unto her, according to the time of life..."*

If you look closely, you will find that the woman never imagined herself giving birth again, considering her age and other factors known to her. But the power of giving unlocked the miraculous on her. And if you read the passage further, you will find that the miracle-child she got grew up but became ill at a time and died. Elisha immediately got to work again to resurrect the child. So, the woman literally got two miracles, without expecting any, in the first place.

Still, like the other two keys, giving remains subservient to the master key because it can sometimes miss the mark due to the motive behind it or the manner in which it is done. In other words, it cannot always guarantee the miraculous. In fact, giving can end up achieving the very opposite of what the giver intends. We have a classic example of this in Acts 8:9-20, *"But there was a certain man, called Simon, which beforetime in the same city used sorcery, and bewitched the people of Samaria, giving out that himself was some great one: To whom they all gave heed, from the least to the greatest, saying, This man is the great power of God. And to him they had regard, because that of long time he had bewitched them with sorceries. But when they believed Philip preaching the things concerning the kingdom of God, and the name of Jesus Christ, they were baptized, both men and women. Then Simon himself believed also: and when he was baptized, he continued with Philip, and wondered, beholding the miracles and signs which were done. Now when the apostles which were at Jerusalem heard that Samaria had received the word of God, they sent unto them Peter and John: Who, when they were come down, prayed for them, that they might receive the Holy Ghost: (For as yet he was fallen upon none of them: only they were baptized in the name of the Lord Jesus.) Then laid they their hands on them, and they received the Holy Ghost. And when Simon saw that through laying on of the apostles' hands the Holy Ghost was given, he offered them money, Saying, Give me also this power, that on whomsoever I lay hands, he may receive the Holy Ghost. But Peter said unto him, Thy money perish with thee, because thou hast thought that the gift of God may be purchased with money."*

Simon the Sorcerer apparently had plenty of ill-gotten money, and he thought he could step into the miraculous like the apostles by doing some giving. What he got instead was a curse because he lacked the real substance (master key) that turns giving into a miracle pathway.

Now, you may say Simon deserved what he got anyway; after all, he had been a sorcerer, whose claim of being converted like other people might have been fabricated. Thus, before examining the master key itself, I want us to see another example of a prominent Israelite who prioritized giving as way of currying God's favor but ended up with an opposite result. This case is particularly important because it gives us a clue of what the master key is and why it is the only assured pathway to the miraculous.

1 Samuel 15:20-23 reads: *"And Saul said unto Samuel, Yea, I have obeyed the voice of the LORD, and have gone the way which the LORD sent me, and have brought Agag the king of Amalek, and have utterly destroyed the Amalekites. But the people took of the spoil, sheep and oxen, the chief of the things which should have been utterly destroyed, to sacrifice unto the LORD thy God in Gilgal. And Samuel said, Hath the LORD as great delight in burnt offerings and sacrifices, as in obeying the voice of the LORD? Behold, to obey is better than sacrifice, and to hearken than the fat of rams.*

For rebellion is as the sin of witchcraft, and stubbornness is as iniquity and idolatry.

Because thou hast rejected the word of the LORD, he hath also rejected thee from being king."

Saul thought he could hoodwink the prophet by alluding to the fact that the animals and other belongings taken from the Amalekites were to be sacrificed to God. But Samuel proved more knowledgeable and discerning by telling him that even if that were true, he and his people had tragically misfired in thinking that giving – even the best of offerings – could supersede God's own ordained pathway to divine favor and supernatural blessings. Saul, therefore ended up losing, where he thought he would have gained because he didn't know what matters most to God.

I believe, by now, you should have begun to see the picture of the master key, as well as understanding why you and I cannot do without it.

6

MASTER KEY TO OPERATING IN THE MIRACULOUS

"God's Word does not merely impart information; it actually creates life. It is not only descriptive; it is effective too, God speaking is God acting." - **Michael Horton**

"For as the rain comes down, and the snow from heaven, and do not return there, but water the earth, and make it bring forth and bud, that it may give seed to the sower and bread to the eater, So shall My word be that goes forth from My mouth; It shall not return to Me void, but it shall accomplish what I please, and it shall prosper in the thing for which I sent it." **(Isaiah 55:10-11)**

"For the word of God is living and powerful, and sharper than any two-edged sword..." **(Hebrews 4:12)**

God's Word is the master key and the assured pathway to

the miraculous. Indeed, no amount of praying, fasting, praising or giving can equal the power of God's Word in opening the floodgates of the miraculous upon our lives. The Word of God is an all-encompassing and all-purpose medication that has been specially packaged by God Himself to meet every need we may have.

Have you ever wondered why God, in telling Joshua what he needed to succeed and prosper in life, said: *"This book of the law shall not depart out of thy mouth; but thou shalt meditate therein day and night, that thou mayest observe to do according to all that is written therein: for then thou shalt make thy way prosperous, and then thou shalt have good success"* (Joshua 1:8)? Have you wondered why God did not tell him to pray hard, praise more or give much, in order to succeed?

You see, prayer is powerful, praise is awesome and giving is effective but a life that will be truly successful, victorious and will consistently enjoy the miraculous is a life that is thoroughly saturated with the Word of God. I will give you detailed reasons why God's Word is the master key and the assured pathway to the miraculous in a short while. Before then, let me ask another question. Have you wondered why Jesus Christ, in confronting and overcoming the devil at the beginning of His ministry did not merely rely on the prayer and fasting He had just concluded (Matthew 4:1-11)? In fact, does it not amaze you that the devil had to come immediately after the marathon prayer and fasting He had just undergone? Well, that in itself, tells a lot about how prayer works.

So, what did Jesus use in getting the devil out of His way? The Word of God. Check each of the three temptations that the enemy brought to derail His ministry, and you would find that He had to continuously refer to the Word to silence and resist the enemy. That tells you how much Satan himself fears and bows before the power of the Word. And I can tell you categorically that the reason many believers today continue to cringe and crumble before temptations, satanic manipulations and all kinds of affliction is not because they do not know how to pray, fast, give or praise; it is because they are deficient in the knowledge, assimilation and application of the Word!

WHY GOD'S WORD IS THE MASTER KEY

Now, let's return to the main question here. Why is God's Word the assured pathway or master key to the miraculous?

1. God stands by His Word.

In Isaiah 55:8-11, He says: *"For as the rain cometh down, and the snow from heaven, and returneth not thither, but*

81

watereth the earth, and maketh it bring forth and bud, that it may give seed to the sower, and bread to the eater: So shall my word be that goeth forth out of my mouth: it shall not return unto me void, but it shall accomplish that which I please, and it shall prosper in the thing whereto I sent it."

This is an uncommon and unprecedented promise of God that elevates His Word above every other key to the miraculous. He is simply giving a strong assurance that as you read His Word, you can hold Him accountable to fulfil every promise your spirit grasps in it in your life. He is saying that just as the rain and the snow fall and enrich the ground, making it unfailingly yield and blossom, so will His Word certainly cause your life to flourish.

You will never find God saying that prayer, praise, giving or any other pathway you may think of will not come to Him empty. And indeed, we know that many prayers, praises and acts of giving are empty before God. But here is God saying that this can never happen with His Word. Every Word that God ministers to your spirit through His Spirit; or more precisely – every Word of God concerning your life that your spirit is able to receive and act upon – must accomplish the purpose for which it was sent. Whether the Word is about grace, healing, strength, success, prosperity, breakthrough, conception, promotion, peace, joy – whatever it is – it must prosper in your life and prevail over every circumstance.

This means that every promise and declaration concerning your situation that your spirit is able to assimilate and appropriate is bound to yield results in your life. What makes you continually function in the realm of the miraculous therefore is the volume of the Word of God in your spirit. Jesus clearly declared that the Word of God is Spirit and life (John 6:63). In other words, the Word of God is a life-giving Spirit. Remember the role that the Spirit of God played in the creation of the world, as we examined earlier? When the Spirit of God gets into action, miracles, wonders and transformations are bound to occur.

Therefore every Word of God that connects with your spirit must effect the miraculous in your life and through you. I am especially confident of this because *"God is not a man, that he should lie; neither the son of man, that he should repent: hath he said, and shall he not do it? or hath he spoken, and shall he not make it good?"* (Numbers 23:19).

2. Only God's Word remains unchanging.

Isaiah 40:8 says, *"The grass withereth, the flower fadeth: but the word of our God shall stand for ever."* Jesus also confirmed this, saying: *"Heaven and earth shall pass away, but my words shall not pass away.* " (Matthew 24:35). This, again, is what makes God's Word the assured pathway and master key to the miraculous. Because it is from God Himself, it remains unchanging and unfailing, regardless of time or environment. You can move from one place to another and the Word of God will still work for you same way. Its truth and efficacy remain the same, whether it is day or night. From generation to generation, mankind has depended on the same Word of God and it continues to achieve the same miraculous effects it says it will accomplish.

Every other key or pathway varies according to time and environment. Take prayer for example, it is often worded according to status, time and situations. Let me explain this better. The pattern of prayer in African churches is different from what you have in European churches. In fact, even in America, the pattern of praise and worship among the Black community is different from what you have among our Caucasian brothers and sisters. So, culture, environment, status, age and sometimes even gender affect the nature, tenor and focus of prayer, praise and giving.

However, it is the same Word of God that everyone studies, meditates and acts upon and it performs exactly what God says it will perform in the life of anyone that receives it into their spirit. Whether you are Black or

White, African or American, rich or poor, male or female, God's Word is the same for everyone and will do what it promises to do according to how you receive it into your spirit. You do not, for instance, have to run from Africa to America for the Word of God on prosperity to work for you. Wherever you are, whoever you are, God's Word is programmed to transform, prosper, enrich and nourish your life and that is the exact result it will achieve. This is why 2 Peter 1:19 describes God's Word as *"a more sure word of prophecy; whereunto ye do well that ye take heed, as unto a light that shineth in a dark place, until the day dawn, and the day star arise in your hearts."*

3. It is God's Word that makes other keys effective.

Now, this is very serious. The Word, on its own, can serve its specified purpose and produce results, even without prayer, praise or giving. Do not get me wrong, please; these other keys are very important and necessary. But the Word does not have to have them available to serve its purpose. Let me give you a good example, for better understanding. Acts 10:44-45 reads, *"While Peter yet spake these words, the Holy Ghost fell on all them which heard the word. And they of the circumcision which believed were astonished, as many as came with Peter, because that on the Gentiles also was poured out the gift of the Holy Ghost."*

Now, do you see the point I am making here? How were

85

you taught to receive the baptism of the Holy Spirit? By prayer. How did the disciples themselves receive the Holy Spirit? They spent several days praying and tarrying. But here we have Gentiles who received the Holy Spirit by just listening to the Word with rapt attention for some minutes. That tells you the "standalone" efficacy of the Word. Jesus Himself affirmed this when He said, *"Now ye are clean through the word which I have spoken unto you."* (John 15:3). He did not say they were cleansed by the prayer, praise or giving they had offered but just by the Word!

On the contrary, no other key can be effective without the backing of the Word. The Bible says that *"God is a Spirit: and they that worship him must worship him in spirit and in truth."* (John 4:24). What truth is Christ referring to here? The truth of God's Word. Our God is a God of order and standards and therefore cannot be worshipped, persuaded or impressed haphazardly. Every other thing we do – praying, fasting, praising or giving must align with the dictates of His Word. This is why every other key or pathway to the miraculous becomes empty and powerless without the Word of God.

Prayer, as we have seen, can work wonders; but, in reality, what makes prayer powerful is not eloquence of language, length of time or amount of tears – what makes it effective is its alignment with God's Word. I agree that the name of Jesus is powerful and is above every other name (Philippians 2:9-11). I agree that *"the name of the LORD is a strong tower: the righteous runneth into it, and is safe."* (Proverbs 18:10). Yet, the Scripture clearly states that God has exalted His Word above His name (Psalm 138:2). This means that you can know all the names of God and still pray or praise amiss, without the richness of God's Word in Your Spirit.

Let me make this even clearer. In a previous chapter, we examined our identity, positioning, power, privileges, provisions, anointing and authority in God's Kingdom. How do we get to know all these? It is through God's Word. And it is as you understand who you are, what you possess and where you are meant to be that you are driven to pray, praise and give, and to do so effectively.

Moreover, what constitutes the content of your prayer? What will you say to move God without His Word? Observe the prayer of Mary in Luke 1:38, *"Behold the handmaid of the Lord; be it unto me according to thy word."* This is one of the simplest but most effective prayers that anyone can pray. Mary had received God's Word into her spirit, and she asked that the Word come into manifestation in her life. It was a similar approach that David adopted in 1 Chronicles 17:23-27: *"Therefore now, LORD, let the thing that thou hast spoken concerning thy servant and concerning his house be established for ever, and do as thou hast said. Let it even be established, that thy name may be magnified for ever, saying, The LORD of hosts is the God of Israel, even a God to Israel: and let the house of David thy servant be established before thee. For thou, O my God, hast told thy servant that thou wilt build him an house: therefore thy servant hath found in his heart to pray before thee. And now, LORD, thou art God, and hast promised this goodness unto thy servant: Now therefore let it please thee to bless the house of thy servant, that it may be before thee for ever: for thou blessest, O LORD, and it shall be blessed for ever."*

This is the kind of prayer that moves God and shakes the kingdom of Satan. You must know what has been said concerning your life and destiny and stand on it. And only the Word of God can reveal this to you. Otherwise, ordinary emotions and tears will achieve nothing. This is why God says that *"My people are destroyed for lack of knowledge"* (Hosea 4:6) - not lack of prayer, praise or giving. Many people pray, fast, speak in tongues, praise and give yet their lives remain the same because they do these things in ignorance or complete defiance of God's Word.

Take note of this today – it is your conformity and alignment with God's Word that validates everything else you do before God. It is being obedient to what the

Word says. This is why God told Moses, *"Be sure that you make everything according to the pattern I have shown you here on the mountain."* (Exodus 25:40). This means that anything outside of that would be vain and void. Same applies to every other key or pathway you use in seeking the miraculous. Moreover, it is your spirit's saturation with God's Word that will enrich your prayers, enhance your praise, and empower your giving. It is what will give you confidence before the Throne and Grace and sharpen your authority against the kingdom of darkness!

4.   God's Word cannot be hindered.

Prayers, praise and giving can be hindered or rendered ineffective but not so with God's Word. Whatever God says He will do will be done. Nothing can withstand or neutralize the force and power of the Word. Jeremiah 23:29 says, *"Is not my word like as a fire? saith the LORD; and like a hammer that breaketh the rock in pieces?"* And Hebrews 4:12 affirms, *"For the word of God is quick, and powerful, and sharper than any twoedged sword..."*

In Daniel 10:12-13, we find a proof that prayer can be hindered, *"Then said he unto me, Fear not, Daniel: for from the first day that thou didst set thine heart to understand, and to chasten thyself before thy God, thy words were heard, and I am come for thy words. But the prince of the kingdom of Persia withstood me one and twenty days..."* Compare this with what Paul said in 2 Timothy 2:9, *"Wherein I suffer trouble, as an evil doer, even unto bonds; but the word of God is not bound."*

Again, despite the initial prevalence of evils and the works of darkness in Ephesus, the Bible says *"So mightily grew the word of God and prevailed"* (Acts 19:20). That is the course of the Word of God. It is always programmed and packaged by God to prevail. As long as you saturate your life with it and stick by faith with its stipulations and promises, it must increasingly expand and prevail over every challenge, sickness, difficulty or every other contrary situation that may be contending against your life and destiny. And it must surely prevail over every issue that you declare it upon.

5. God's Word is the seedbed of every miracle.

Miracles, as we already know, are divine interventions that are meant to enforce God's will. God's will and His Word are intertwined. This is why miracles are often preceded by divine declarations. If you recall the miracles from the Bible that we chronicled earlier, you would find the predominance of God's Word in their performance. In many of the cases, no prayer or praise was involved, yet the miracles occurred, as God's people acted based on faith in God's Word.

Beginning with the miracle of creation, Hebrews 11:3

says, *"Through faith we understand that the worlds were framed by the word of God, so that things which are seen were not made of things which do appear."* This is why we noted that the Word of God is active and life-giving Spirit. As God spoke the Word, it immediately activated whatever God wanted to manifest. In essence, God performed the first miracle by declaring His word upon the darkness and emptiness that pervaded the earth: - *"And God said, Let there be light: and there was light."* (Genesis 1:3). And till today and forever, wherever the Word of God is declared in faith over darkness, light takes over (John 1:5).

Whether it was the crossing of the Red Sea, the demolition of Jericho walls or the turning of water into wine, you will find the dominance of Word. It's either the Word was declared or obeyed. In the parting of the Red Sea, for instance, God simply told Moses to stretch his rod over the sea – and he obeyed, and even without praying any special prayer, the sea submitted to the authority of the Word. In the case of water being turned to wine, Jesus' mother – who was already familiar with the irresistible power of God's Word - simply told the servants: *"Whatsoever he saith unto you, do it."* (John 2:5).

In the miracle of Peter catching a massive haul of fishes, he declared, *"Master, we have toiled all the night, and have taken nothing: nevertheless at thy word I will let down the net.* "(Luke 5:5). Also, in the miracle of Peter walking on the sea, we are told, *"And Peter answered him and said, Lord, if it be thou, bid me come unto thee on the water. And he said, Come. And when Peter was come down out of the ship, he walked on the water, to go to Jesus."* (Matthew 14:28-29)

That is the secret to the miraculous – get the Word and you are good to go. This is indispensable for the miraculous. Fortunately, as we have already seen, God's Word contains all the miracles and promises of God that apply to every situation or challenge that will ever confront you in life. This is why familiarity with God's Word, through constant reading and meditation, is critical to operating in the miraculous.

The Word is your password. Get the Word and latch on to it in faith, till you see the manifestation!

6. Miracles based on God's Word last forever

When people receive random miracles, for which they cannot personally pinpoint the basis in God's Word, they are sometimes in doubt of the authenticity of what they have received and how long it will last. Some are particularly worried that Satan will come and take it away from them. Take the example of the woman that received her miracle child through her hospitality towards Elisha. When the child grew and later died, her first expression to Elisha was, *"Did I desire a son of my lord? did I not say, Do not deceive me?"* (2 Kings 4:28). This shows that she had always considered the miracle to be too good to be true and never really personally owned it.

On the contrary, Word-based miracles are often prepackaged with the assurance of genuineness and permanence – two of the characteristics of God's Word. When you understand, through the Scripture, your entitlements or covenant birthrights as God's child, as well as the faithfulness and the immutability of your everlasting heavenly Father, you can never be scared that your miracles will be short-lived. You will continually bask in the confidence that you have received your miracles from *"he that openeth, and no man shutteth; and shutteth, and no man openeth"* (Revelation 3:7).

It was this confidence that made Apostle Paul to declare: *"For I know whom I have believed, and am persuaded that he is able to keep that which I have committed unto him against that day."* (2 Timothy 1:12). You need such confidence to continually enjoy the manifold blessings of the miraculous life.

7

GETTING THE WORD IN YOUR SPIRIT

"Absorb the Word into your system by dwelling on it, pondering it, going over it again and again in your mind, considering it from many different angles, until it becomes part of you." - **Nancy Leigh DeMoss**

*"Let the word of Christ dwell in you richly in all wisdom, teaching and admonishing one another in psalms and hymns and spiritual songs, singing with grace in your hearts to the Lord." (**Colossians 3:16**)*

*"Your words were found, and I ate them, and Your word was to me the joy and rejoicing of my heart..." (**Jeremiah 15:16**)*

The renowned evangelist, Gipsy Smith, once told of a man who said he had experienced no transformation from the Bible, although he had "gone through it several times." The evangelist simply replied him, "Let it go through you once, then you will tell a different story!"

This is the exact prescription that majority of believers need today. We sometimes wonder why God's Word is not prospering and producing the expected results in our lives. The reason, most times, is not because we do not know the Word but because the Word has not been assimilated into our spirit. In other words, what we have is just head knowledge. We are not really convinced and fully persuaded about it enough to make it penetrate and dominate the very core of our being.

Recall that It was God that brought the Israelites out of Egypt and promised to plant them in a land flowing with milk and honey. How come this promise did not manifest for most of them? Why did they, instead, perish in the wilderness? Hebrews 4:1-2 has the answer: *"Let us therefore fear, lest, a promise being left us of entering into his rest, any of you should seem to come short of it. For unto us was the gospel preached, as well as unto them: but the word preached did not profit them, not being mixed with faith in them that heard it."*

The Word did not profit the people because they took it "with a pinch of salt". They did not take it seriously enough to get it implanted in their spirit.

UNDERSTANDING THE SPIRIT FACTOR

So, why the emphasis on the Word being in our spirit? Well, you have to recall again that man was created in the image of God. Therefore as God is Triune – God the Father, God the Son and God the Holy Spirit – humans are also tripartite beings. We are comprised of spirit, soul and body. Put simply, every human is a spirit that has a soul and lives in a body. As proof of our tripartite nature, 1 Thessalonians 5:23 says, *"And the very God of peace sanctify you wholly; and I pray God your whole spirit and soul and body be preserved blameless unto the coming of our Lord Jesus Christ."*

Essentially, each of us is primarily a spirit being, and it is with our spirit that we are able to connect to the spirit realm and also communicate with God because He is Spirit. However, what makes us to be able to live on earth is our body; while our soul – which consists of our mind, conscience, will, intellect and emotions – is what acts as the "middleman" between our body and our spirit.

In this role of connecting with both our spirit and our body, our soul feeds each of these two components with what it receives from the other. Now, this is where the epic battle, described in Galatians 5:17 comes in. *"For the flesh desires what is contrary to the Spirit, and the Spirit what is contrary to the flesh. They are in conflict with each other…"* (NIV). Our body, being in the world and very vulnerable to the wiles of Satan, wants to download as many fleshly things as possible from the world into our soul (mostly through our sense organs), to be fed into our spirit. This way, our spirit can be polluted and brought under the control of the devil. On the other hand, our spirit, which is more attuned to God, wants to download things from the Holy Spirit of God into our soul, so that our body and our life on earth in general can be made to obey the will of God.

This is also where we become accountable for the outcome of our life on earth. With our soul, we constantly make choices that determine who wins the battle between our flesh and spirit – and ultimately between the devil and the Spirit of God in our life. It is for this reason that the Bible says, *"Dearly beloved, I beseech you as strangers and pilgrims, abstain from fleshly lusts, which war against the soul."* (1 Peter 2:11). And also, *"Walk in the Spirit, and ye shall not fulfil the lust of the flesh."* (Galatians 5:16). In other words, we must choose to allow our spirit (as empowered by the Holy Spirit of God) to have the upper hand over the cravings of our flesh.

WHAT ARE YOU FEEDING YOUR SPIRIT?

This brings us back to our main subject here – downloading the Word into our Spirit. It is with our body, or more precisely, the sense organs of our body that we get the Word. We might read or hear it; or it might even be shown to us by dreams or visions. But it is what we decide to do with the Word (through our soul) that determines whether it gets to our spirit or not. And since it is with our spirit we communicate with God, it is what we have in there that we present to Him and He responds to.

"Deep calleth unto deep" (Psalm 42:7). God does not dwell in our flesh; He dwells in our spirit and therefore only connects with expressions that emanate from our spirit. This is why I mentioned that it is not our tears that move God; what moves Him is the richness of the Word which we have allowed the Holy Spirit to download to our spirit. It was this understanding that spurred Paul the Apostle to exhort, *"Let the word of Christ dwell in you richly in all wisdom…"* (Colossians 3:16).

Sadly, what many believers often do with the Word is to, at most, let it stay in the most outer part of our soul, which is our sensory or short-term memory. It does not permeate our entire soul, much less penetrating our spirit and saturating it. So, we only end up with memorized recitations of the letters of the Word that communicate nothing to God nor add any value to our lives – *"for the letter killeth, but the spirit giveth life"* (2 Corinthians 3:6).

The point here is that the reason the Word seems not to

be effecting the expected miracles in the lives of many of us is not because God has started to lie or that His Word is no longer effective; it is because we are not telling Him what He wants to hear and how He wants to hear it. He challenges us in Isaiah 43:26, *"Put me in remembrance: let us plead together: declare thou, that thou mayest be justified."* But how do we do this without communicating in His language?

Pay attention to what Paul says in 1 Corinthians 2:4-14: *"And my speech and my preaching was not with enticing words of man's wisdom, but in demonstration of the Spirit and of power: That your faith should not stand in the wisdom of men, but in the power of God. Howbeit we speak wisdom among them that are perfect: yet not the wisdom of this world, nor of the princes of this world, that come to nought: But we speak the wisdom of God in a mystery, even the hidden wisdom, which God ordained before the world unto our glory: Which none of the princes of this world knew: for had they known it, they would not have crucified the Lord of glory. But as it is written, Eye hath not seen, nor ear heard, neither have entered into the heart of man, the things which God hath prepared for them that love him. But God hath revealed them unto us by his Spirit: for the Spirit searcheth all things, yea, the deep things of God. For what man knoweth the things of a man, save the spirit of man which is in him? even so the things of God knoweth no man, but the Spirit of God. Now we have received, not the spirit of the world, but the spirit which is of God; that we might know the things that are freely given to us of God. Which things also we speak, not in the words which man's wisdom teacheth, but which the Holy Ghost teacheth; comparing spiritual things with spiritual. But the natural man receiveth not the things of the Spirit of God: for they are foolishness unto him: neither can he know them, because they are spiritually discerned."*

This is a full picture of the thinking and communication system of the spiritual realm. He says the language is not about the grammar, diction or vocabulary of the earthly realm; nor is it about the sharpness of our memory in reciting the letters of the Scripture. That is not what unravel and unleashes the power of God. What does is the seamless communion between the Word and our spirit and between our spirit and the Spirit of God.

Now, I need to briefly explain something, which you might have prominently observed in the above passage. This is the variation in the cases in which the letter "s" is set in spirit. This is done generally in the Scripture to differentiate the Holy Spirit (capital S) from the human or any other kind of spirit (lower case s). You should therefore understand that, in saying that the Word should settle in your sprit, I am referring to your human spirit and not the Holy Spirit. The Holy Spirit and the Word are always perfectly in agreement. As 1 John 5:7

says, *"For there are three that bear record in heaven, the Father, the Word, and the Holy Ghost: and these three are one."*

So, it is very clear. The Father and the Holy Spirit are in perpetual unity with the Word. You are the one they are waiting for to align with them in your spirit, so that the miraculous can begin in your life. As I already told you, everything you need to succeed, prosper, prevail in life are in the Word. Every miracle, solution or answer you can think of is already in the Word. They may not be glaring to the natural eyes but as you allow the Holy Spirit who searches "the deep things of God" to illuminate them to your spirit, you begin the process of downloading miracles into your life.

Bear in mind that I am talking about your regenerated spirit because the natural spirit can never understand the language of God's Spirit. So, I am assuming that you are born again. If you are not, then there is so much you will be missing out on. Therefore, I enjoin you to briefly close your eyes, as you yield your spirit to Jesus Christ, for Him to take over your life and become your Savior and Lord. Acknowledge yourself as a sinner, who needs the cleansing of the blood of Jesus and invite Him into your heart to abide with you forevermore.

If you have done that, I congratulate you. The Spirit of God now indwells you to empower your spirit in the pathway of righteousness and the miraculous.

ALIGNING YOUR SPIRIT WITH THE WORD FOR THE MIRACULOUS

How then do you get the Word settled and productive in your spirit? Let us revisit God's admonition to Joshua: *"This book of the law shall not depart out of thy mouth; but thou shalt meditate therein day and night, that thou mayest observe to do according to all that is written therein: for then thou shalt make thy way prosperous, and then thou shalt have good success."* (Joshua 1:8-9).

God's prescription is that you take studying and meditating on the Scripture seriously, not casually. It is something that will require you to consciously create time for God's Word; to prioritize it above the time you spend on TV, social media, hanging out and other fleshly amusements (see Job 23:12). And it must involve full attention from your sensory organs and your soul. It is with your eyes that you study the Word and it is with your ears that you listen to it, whether in church or on tape. However, it is with your soul that you meditate on it and look for its connections with the different areas of your life.

Meditation is so important as it helps the Word to permeate your soul and consequently your spirit. In the words of George Muller, "As the outward man is not fit for work for any length of time unless he eats, so it is with the inner man. What is the food for the inner man? Not prayer, but the Word of God – not the simple reading of the Word of God, so that it only passes through our minds, just as water runs through a pipe. No, we must consider what we read, ponder over it, and apply it to our hearts." Charles Spurgeon adds, "Oh, to be bathed in a text of Scripture, and to let it be sucked up into your very soul, till it saturates your heart! Set your heart upon God's Word! Let your whole nature be plunged into it as a cloth into a dye!

The frequency of meditation is also stated by God – "day and night", all-day long. It is as you continue to meditate on God's Word that the Holy Spirit begins to illuminate it for your spirit man to grasp. And then your spirit begins to bear witness with the Holy Spirit that the Word is indeed YOURS. With this claim of ownership, the prospering and miraculous power embedded in the Word and the process of manifestation is activated!

Note however that the entire process, from the receiving of the Word by your senses to meditation and reception in your spirit does not necessarily have to take a day or even an hour to accomplish. It could be in a jiffy, as quickly as your mind is ready to receive the Word with faith. I showed you an example earlier on this concerning the household of Cornelius. The Holy Spirit fell on them, right as they paid rapt, faith-filled attention to the Word. Instantly, their bodies, souls and spirits yielded to the illumination of the Spirit of God and they got an unprecedented divine visitation.

The same still happens today. A minister may be preaching or a personal study of the Word and the soul is so aligned to the revelations that the Holy Spirit releases, such that the illumination of the Spirit begins to penetrate your own spirit and you immediately claim the Word to be meant for you. This way, the Word is settled in your spirit and your spirit galvanizes your entire being in prayer of faith to call out to God to do as He has said. And as you continue waiting expectantly with faith in your heart, the Lord Himself will perform that He has said!

In the book, *Pleasures Evermore: The Life-Changing Power of Knowing God*, Sam Storms offers the following insightful tips for getting the Word into your spirit in preparation for the miraculous:

1. *Prepare. Issues of posture, time and place are secondary, but not unimportant. The only rule would be: do whatever is most conducive to concentration.*

2. *Peruse. Read, repeat the reading, write it out, then re-write it.*

3. *Picture. Apply your imagination and senses to the truth of the text. Envision yourself personally engaged in the relationship or encounter or experience of which the text speaks.*

4. *Ponder. Reflect on the truth of the Word; brood over the truth of the text; absorb it, soak it in, as you turn it over in your mind.*

5. *Pray. At some point take the truth as the Holy Spirit has illuminated it and pray it back to God whether in petition, thanksgiving, or intercession.*

6. *Personalize. Where possible, according to sound principles of biblical interpretation, replace proper names and proper pronouns with your own name.*

7. *Praise. Worship the Lord for who He is and what He has done and how it has been revealed in Scripture.*

8. *Practice. Commit yourself to doing what the Word commands.*

Now, that you are fire up to begin to operate in the miraculous and enjoy your miracles, let's look at one more crucial step.

8

ACTIVATING THE MIRACULOUS BY FAITH

"Faith sees the invisible, believes the unbelievable, and receives the impossible." - **Corrie Ten Boom**

"…Believe in the LORD your God, and you shall be established; believe His prophets, and you shall prosper." – ***(2 Chronicles 20:20)***

"But without faith it is impossible to please Him, for he who comes to God must believe that He is, and that He is a rewarder of those who diligently seek Him." – ***(Hebrews 11:6)***

Now that you have got the Word of God settled in your spirit and constantly breathing it forth unto the Spirit of God for the manifestation, you are set for the outpouring of the miraculous. But you must intensify the tempo of faith with which you have received the Word into your Spirit in the first place. You must step it up towards activating your miracle.

Hebrews 11:1 says, *"Now faith is the substance of things hoped for, the evidence of things not seen."* Your faith is what connects you to the physical manifestations of your miracles. What faith does is that it goes into the realm of the spirit or the supernatural, lay hold on the promises of God that are in the word of God and bring them to the believer in physical form. *"(As it is written, I have made thee a father of many nations,) before him whom he believed, even God, who quickeneth the dead, and calleth those things which be not as though they were."* (Romans 4:17).

It is through faith that we have access to God and all the things that are available in the supernatural realm. However, since faith without works is dead (James 2:14-17), you must actively demonstrate this activating faith by letting the Word in your spirit become the engine that drives your thoughts, words and actions. Everything about you must reflect your faith in the faithfulness and omnipotence of the Almighty God to fulfil everything He has said concerning you, in His word. As you continue to demonstrate faith in the Word, you automatically open yourself up for the miraculous. Remember that Jesus Christ is the Word of God (John 1:1-3).

ACCELERATING MIRACULOUS MANIFESTATIONS

One key way to accelerate the manifestation of the miraculous is through your declaration of the Word in prayer and in your daily life. 2 Corinthians 4:13 says, *"We having the same spirit of faith, according as it is written, I believed, and therefore have I spoken; we also believe, and therefore speak."* The implication here is that it is impossible for you to believe the Word of God and not declare it. When the light of God's Word shines upon your heart as a revelation, you cannot be quiet. No matter how introverted or reserved you are, when the light of God's Word shines into your spirit - you cannot remain quiet!

Faith is, therefore, the substance of the things we hope, which we must speak in faith into existence, notwithstanding how we are feeling at the moment. This is especially necessary to counter the "fiery darts" of doubt that the enemy may want to bring to you through negative thoughts and circumstances.

As a believer, in seeing the manifestation of your miracles, your words are not just important, they are vital. In Mark 11:23, Jesus says, *"For verily I say unto you, That whosoever shall say unto this mountain, Be thou removed, and be thou cast into the sea; and shall not doubt in his heart, but shall believe that those things which he saith shall come to pass; he shall have whatsoever he saith."* The assurance that you will have whatever you say should inspire you to make faith-driven declarations concerning your life and situations, as often as possible.

As we have already seen, all the miracles you will ever need is already promised and demonstrated in God's Word. These miracles are only waiting for you to activate and bring them into existence. Therefore, as God used the power of the Word to call forth whatever He wanted into the universe, you too must, by faith, call forth the manifestation of the Word in every aspect of your life.

What has been said concerning your life and destiny? That you will prosper and be in health, even as your soul prospers (3 John 2). Declare, and declare it often. What has been said concerning your marriage and family? That you will *"eat the labour of thine hands: happy shalt thou be, and it shall be well with thee. Thy wife shall be as a fruitful vine by the sides of thine house: thy children like olive plants round about thy table... Yea, thou shalt see thy children's children"* (Psalms 128:3-6). Declare it. What has been said about your work and finances? That *"the LORD shall open unto thee his good treasure, the heaven to give the rain unto thy land in his season, and to bless all the work of thine hand: and thou shalt lend unto many...and thou shalt not borrow."* (Deuteronomy 28:12). Declare it.

What has been said concerning your healing and health? That *"I will put none of these diseases upon thee, which I have brought upon the Egyptians: for I am the LORD that healeth thee."* (Exodus 15:26). Declare it. What has God said concerning your children? *"And all thy children shall be taught of the LORD; and great shall be the peace of thy children."* (Isaiah 54:13). Call it forth. What has God said concerning your professional and career success? *"The LORD shall make thee the head, and not the tail; and thou shalt be above only, and thou shalt not be beneath."* (Deuteronomy 28:13).

What has God said regarding your protection? *"Surely he shall deliver thee from the snare of the fowler, and from the noisome pestilence... Thou shalt not be afraid for the terror by night; nor for the arrow that flieth by day; Nor for the pestilence that walketh in darkness; nor for the destruction that wasteth at noonday. A thousand shall fall at thy side, and ten thousand at thy right hand; but it shall not come nigh thee."* (Psalms 91:3-7). Make it a reality. What has He said about premature death in your life? *"I shall not die, but live, and declare the works of the LORD."* (Psalms 118:17). Call it forth.

On and on, you must declare, until the manifestations come and only the will of God prevails in your life. As we have clearly established, the Word is the basis for our miracle. This means that without the Word, there can be no miracle to enforce or call into existence. Therefore, you must guard against the enemy, making you forget the Word, especially when things seem to be contrary in the physical realm. Only the Word that is forever established in heaven can set things right again; so you must never let it "depart out of thy mouth."

Because you were made in the image of God and share in His power of creativity, whatever you declare – according to God's Word - will come into manifestation. Your declarations will ultimately lead to your reality. It is not magic; it is what God Himself says, *"As truly as I live, saith the LORD, as ye have spoken in mine ears, so will I do to you"* (Numbers 14:28). God listens to your declarations and will hasten to perform His Word that you declare. *"Then said the LORD unto me, Thou hast well seen: for I will hasten my word to perform it."* (Jeremiah 1:12).

ALL-ROUND POTENCY OF FAITH

In Mark 11:24, Jesus says, *"Therefore I say unto you, What things soever ye desire, when ye pray, believe that ye receive them, and ye shall have them."* Whatever miracles you expect to see or operate in, as you make your prayer declarations, back them up with the firm belief that they will manifest, and you will see them manifesting.

One of the beautiful things about faith, as reflected in

the above promise, is that it works the same in all realms of life and for all our needs. By saying whatsoever you desire, believe, Jesus is simply saying that it is the same faith you exercised in getting one of your needs met that you will exercise in getting others. For instance, the same faith you exercised in believing that you had been forgiven and saved is what you use in believing and receiving other blessings from God. The same faith you use in getting your healing is what you need is turning around your finances for good. It is the same faith you use for your breakthrough that you will use for your children's health and divine protection -

In essence, as Bible believers, faith is the currency that we "trade" with - no more, no less!

BUILDING UP YOUR FAITH

Since faith is central to the manifestation of the miraculous in our lives, then we have no choice but to constantly build up our faith. Or simply put – we must develop the spirit of faith. How do we do this? We must continue to expose ourselves to the Word of God, meditate on it and believe in it. Romans 10:17 says, *"So then faith cometh by hearing, and hearing by the word of God."*

Faith is based on what the Word of God says and you cannot believe beyond your knowledge of God's Word.

This is why you need to constantly study the Word of God. I encourage you, beloved believer, build your faith on the Word of God and not on anything else. Only the Word can sustain and strengthen your spirit in faith for the manifestation of the miraculous.

STAND ON THE SURE WORD OF PROPHECY

As we conclude on the amazing journey we have had in exploring the assured pathway to the miraculous, we must revisit and constantly recall the revelation in 2 Peter 1:19, concerning the supreme authority and reliability of God's Word: *"We have also a more sure word of prophecy; whereunto ye do well that ye take heed, as unto a light that shineth in a dark place, until the day dawn, and the day star arise in your hearts"*

More than ever before, we must create time for the study and application of the Word of God, not just because we want miracles, but because we want to operate in the miraculous. Romans 8:19 says, *"For the earnest expectation of the creature waiteth for the manifestation of the sons of God."* Our families, communities, churches and nations are awaiting our manifestation with unlimited divine power to transform lives for God.

Since we know we have a more sure Word of Prophecy, we cannot continue to ignorantly wait for others to prophesy into our lives when God has already done so.

Everything we need for life and godliness, for miracles and to operate in the miraculous is in the Word. Every prophecy we need concerning our lives and destinies are already packaged in the Word for us. Our duty is to search them out. As Proverbs 25: 2 says, *"It is the glory of God to conceal a thing: but the honor of kings is to search out a matter."*

I believe in the prophetic ministry but I believe more in the more sure Word of Prophecy. And as the Bible says, we will do well for ourselves, our families, our communities, our churches and, indeed, our generation if we take heed to it.

Made in the USA
Coppell, TX
24 June 2024

33884826R00075